Image Processing

A Management
Perspective

Image Processing
A Management
Perspective

George M. Hall

Trademarks

DEC, DECimage	Digital Equipment Corporation
Kodak, Ektra	Eastman Kodak Company
Epcot Center	Walt Disney Company
Workflo	FileNet Corporation
IBM, Image Plus, PS/2	International Business Machines Corporation
Lotus 1-2-3	Lotus Development Corporation
Windows 3.0	Microsoft Corporation
InfoImage, Unisys	Unisys Corporation
Wang Integrated Image System (WIIS),	Wang Laboratories, Inc.

FIRST EDITION
FIRST PRINTING

© 1991 by **McGraw-Hill, Inc.**.

Printed in the United States of America. All rights reserved. The publisher takes no responsibility for the use of any of the materials or methods described in this book, nor for the products thereof.

Library of Congress Cataloging-in-Publication Data

ISBN 0-07-157746-7(H)

For information about other McGraw-Hill materials, call 1-800-2-MCGRAW in the U.S. In other countries call your nearest McGraw-Hill office.

Vice President and Editorial Director: Larry Hager
Book Editor: Andrew Yoder
Production: Katherine G. Brown
Book Design: Jaclyn J. Boone   TPR4

For Anne, Berry,
Barry and Laura

Contents

Part IV
Management

Acknowledgments

Many individuals contributed time, material and ideas for this book. They are listed in alphabetical order within an alphabetical listing of their respective companies and organizations. I express my thanks to all of them, and also accept any blame for misrepresented information.

For the Automobile Club of Southern California: Edward Banks, Mary Magee, and C.L. Murray were very helpful. At the Association for Information and Image Management: Marilyn Courtot and Jacqueline Virando deserve recognition—especially for the help in guiding me through the mass of references in their resource center. From Digital Equipment Corporation (DEC): John E. Stohlberg sent much information. With Eastman Kodak: I had the pleasure of working with Robert Freese, Jeanne Eason, Edward Hancock, and Jack Kasperski (special thanks to Jack for going the second mile several times). And at the FileNet Corporation: David Key, Sherry Langford, Denise Palmer, and Donald Schnitter provided many insights into what image processing was all about.

Thanks also go to Jim Lundholm and Richard Sella for sending extensive material on the Internal Revenue Service project, which without a doubt will be the largest automated system of any kind the world has ever ever seen. David Liddell, Tom Scott, and Dennis Spokany of IBM devoted a good part of their time to this project. I especially thank Dennis Spokany who went the second and third mile despite my error in at first seeing a resemblance between him and a Hollywood actor (other than one of the principals in the *Butch Cassidy* film). Without Dennis's help, this book would have floundered—although I nearly drowned in the 2,500 pages of material he sent. He also ensured that I visited the competition early on, an act that led that competition to return the compliment.

At Unisys Corporation: Donna Hoffman, Barry Lurie, and Judith Kraynak Maxfield provided much material and spent a great deal of time on the phone to overcome my ignorance on many details. At Wang Laboratories, Harold Marcpein, Larry Mononen, and Michael Runge cut time out from their busy schedules to enlighten my inadequate understanding of image processing.

Introduction

Image processing is widely used today, but relatively few individuals in both technical and managerial positions of responsibility know much about it. This book aims to close that gap.

The 14 chapters are organized into four parts. Part I includes chapters on perspective, theoretical factors, applied factors, and emerging technology. Part II covers structure and storage, image acquisition and access, and software. Part III covers wherewithal, standardization, security, and legal matters. Part IV then looks at planning, implementation, and systems management. The appendices provide a look at: the various application models, case examples, technical notes, a spreadsheet model for return-on-investment analysis, and the Association for Information and Image Processing.

Still, despite the fascinating, widely-used, but largely unknown technology, the tone and emphasis in the book is on management concerns. Even the technical notes were selected because of their significance for management decisions. The arena of image processing is easy to grasp and for most future users, the technology has become something of a proven science. What is scarce, and the industry readily admits it, is the expertise to apply this technology effectively in specific situations. The accelerating number of installations and new features are outpacing the time necessary to digest what is happening.

So the primary intended audience is the manager who has only a peripheral knowledge of image processing, but who wants to understand its potential and perhaps lay the groundwork for a system. The secondary audience are those individuals who have worked long and hard in the image processing trenches, but who need to surface now and then to review the significance of their commendable labors.

The progress of technology is so furious that between the time the page proofs are completed and the time the book comes off the press, some items in the text will have become outdated. These advances almost always work to the advantage of prospective clients, but they are hell on authors.

Part I

Environment

The term *image processing* implies technological and scientific pursuits. Perhaps the most well-known example was the confirmation of Percival Lowell's hypothesis of the ninth planet Pluto. Professor Clyde W. Tombaugh compared photographs taken on January 23 and 29, 1930. The photographs (FIG. I-1) revealed an unidentified stellar object that did not move in concert with the stars—that object was the sought-after planet.

The same technique is being used today in the attempt to locate a hypothesized tenth planet, albeit this time by computer processing. Another version is used for early detection of cancer, especially on freckled skin. This cancer starts as a spot that resembles a freckle. Hence, by periodically comparing electronic facsimile images of the skin, any new "freckle" that appears is suspect. In all, it is a fascinating and eminently worthwhile technology but, for the moment at least, is secondary to the mainstream commercial interests in image processing. Those interests are exemplified by the stack of record boxes, shown in FIG. I-2, used by the Automobile Club of Southern California insurance processing division in a court case. The weeks it took to gather these records could have been compressed to hours or even minutes if their image processing system had been installed earlier.

Businesses see image processing as a way to process paperwork more efficiently than was possible by microfilm predecessors. Those measures reduce storage space, but cannot meet instant retrieval requirements and are difficult to sort. These inadequacies led to the computer-based alternative of storing electronic facsimile images of documents stored on optical media. These documents are ready for instant retrieval and ad hoc linkage and sorting by any number of simultaneous users on a worldwide basis, if necessary.

The concept is easy to grasp, and individuals unfamiliar with computer science can understand it as readily as experts. Yet behind the obvious simplicity at the user end exists a technology more complex than character-and-number information—what I call *data processing*. Further, that technology is

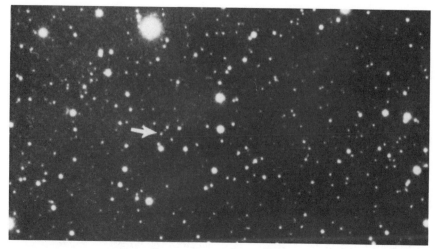

January 23, 1930

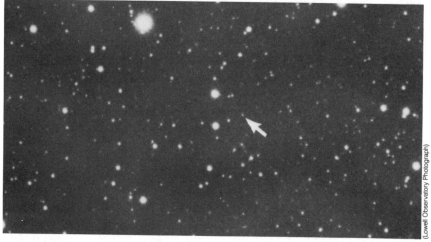

January 29, 1930

Fig. I-1. These are small sections of the discovery plates that show images (those marked) of Lowell's mathematically predicted trans-Neptunian planet afterward named Pluto. *It was found by C. W. Tombaugh on February 18, 1930, while examining these plates.*

more expensive per record and does not entirely eliminate paperwork. Still, the potential savings from reducing the storage space and the number of clerical personnel, plus the strategic advantages that accrue from the ability to retrieve documents instantly, seem to make the investment worthwhile for most operations.

This part of the book, then, provides an overview of the environment in which image processing works and its relationship to data processing. It is written primarily in management terms that lead, where appropriate, to an understanding of salient technological points. It also includes some points on emerging technologies, which suggest an eventual resurgence of scientific applications that are now in the background.

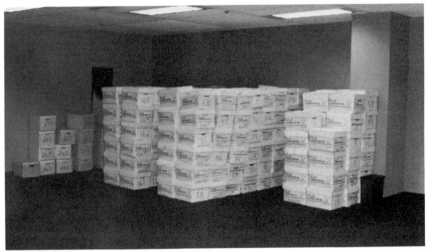

Fig. I-2. An image processing system could have saved the Automobile Club of Southern California much time. These boxes of records were all gathered for a court case.

1

Perspective

This time, like all times, is a very good one,
if we but know what to do with it.

Emerson

A flood of paperwork has inundated most large corporations and government agencies, and is swamping most others. The estimate of existing records is 325 billion, and at least 20 billion are added each year; that is, 90 billion are added and 70 billion are destroyed. Image processing is an electronic means to reduce most of that storage. This processing differs from automated image production, such as computer-assisted drafting (CAD), in that most of the paperwork already exists and the documents that are generated, for the most part, are text files superimposed over images of forms. More importantly, most of the images stored are intended to be read by individuals rather than processed as data by computers; however, attribute information is often added and linked to these records and then processed extensively.

This commercial technology arose from the convergence of several factors, beginning in 1980. Of these factors, the optical disk was the most important. From that point, progress in image processing and the increasing number of new installations can only be described as furious. Perhaps the most intriguing question is: "Why has this phenomenon gone relatively unpublicized?"

The reasons range from the required ten-to-twenty year period that most technologies need to gain public notoriety to the fact that it was initially advocated by professionals outside the mainstream of data processing. Whatever the answer is, image processing is here to stay. This chapter explains why and provides a framework for the balance of the book.

1.1 Coming of age

Automated image processing is more than 25 years old and throughout this time has been used for numerous scientific and medical applications (FIG. 1-1). The problem, however, has been the record length and the resulting high cost of maintaining image data on magnetic disks. A typical image, recorded bit-

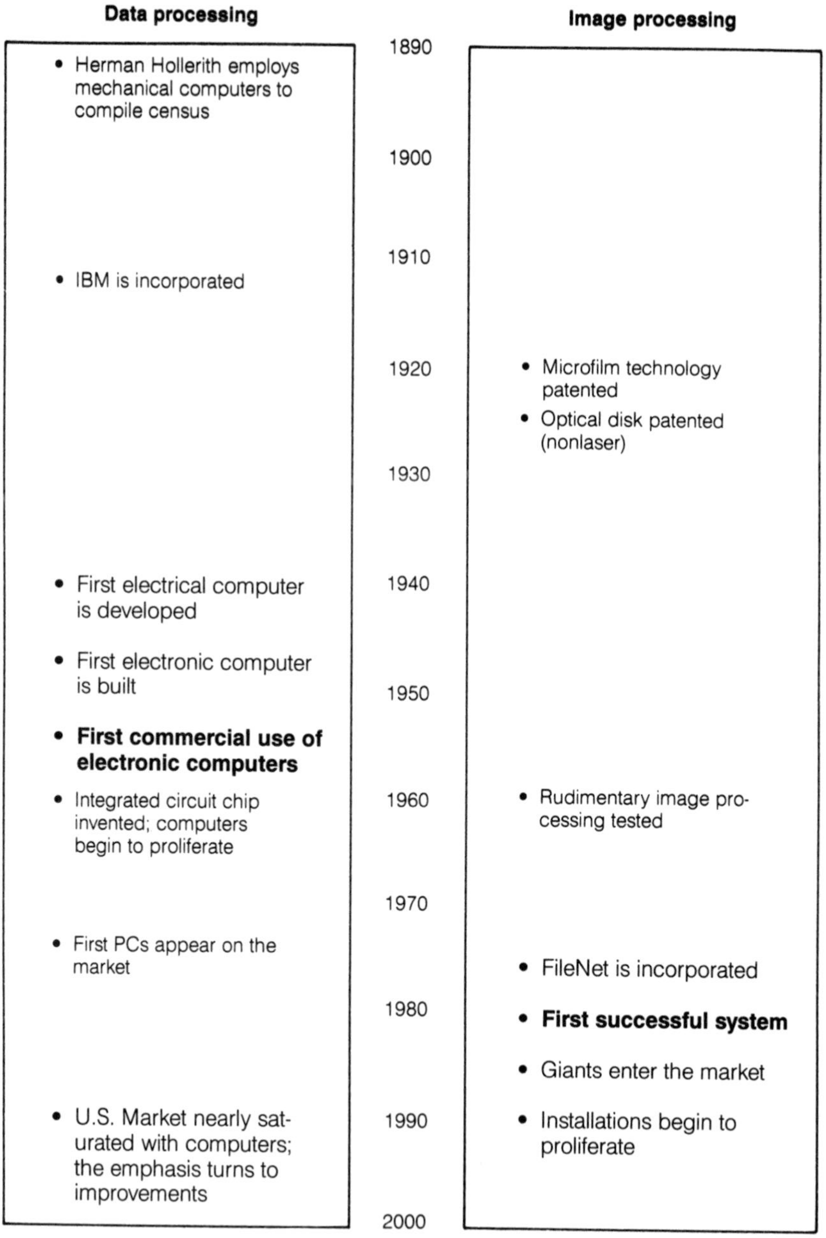

Data processing   **Image processing**

1890
- Herman Hollerith employs mechanical computers to compile census

1900

1910
- IBM is incorporated

1920
- Microfilm technology patented
- Optical disk patented (nonlaser)

1930

1940
- First electrical computer is developed

- First electronic computer is built

1950

- **First commercial use of electronic computers**

- Integrated circuit chip invented; computers begin to proliferate

1960
- Rudimentary image processing tested

1970

- First PCs appear on the market

- FileNet is incorporated

1980
- **First successful system**

- Giants enter the market

- U.S. Market nearly saturated with computers; the emphasis turns to improvements

1990
- Installations begin to proliferate

2000

Fig. 1-1. Image processing technology lags its data processing cousin by several decades, although it is catching up fast. Image processing could become the dominant form of automated systems within 10 years, because most information is still on paper.

for-bit, can use up to one thousand times the storage of a page of text that is recorded character-by-character. Further, many documents must be kept from seven to ten years and some indefinitely; unfortunately, magnetically recorded images start to deteriorate after five years.

The optical disk changed all that. It can store the same data in no more than 10 percent of the space magnetic devices require, at a fraction of the cost, with a reliability that could exceed 30 years. What's more, software algorithms reduce the length of most (but not all) image records by a factor of 10 or more. In short, what formerly cost $100, now only costs pennies. Like pennies, optical disks can remain in circulation much longer than paper money.

Another obstacle, however, had little do with technology. In 1980, most data processing professionals scorned image processing as "electronic micro-filming" confined to the "limited perspective" of records management. With few exceptions, the major computer vendors either ignored the potential or kept it well hidden in research laboratories. The few that attempted to break the ice were largely foreign companies. Although some of the companies pro-duced machines that worked (notably Toshiba) none of them appeared capable of marketing complete systems that were acceptable to management. In stepped Ted Smith.

In 1982, with initial venture capital of only four million dollars, Smith built the FileNet Corporation. By 1984, he and his team of key officers had devel-oped a major product (FIG. 1-2). Within another year they installed their first system. This system supported the investigations of international fund trans-fers at the Security Pacific National Bank, which then required more than 45 million documents. Within five years, that prototype had more than 325 coun-terparts, and FileNet's annual gross grew to $100 million. That isn't much by IBM standards, but then IBM in its first few years (1913-1918) did not do as well proportionally even though it could draw on the experience of a predeces-sor company. FileNet even gained the highest overall ranking in the 1989 Data-pro/Association of Information and Image Management (AIIM) survey of customer satisfaction.

This awoke the giants and a host of lesser companies. By 1990, AIIM had more than 500 vendors as members, including almost every major manufac-turer of computer hardware and telecommunications. These include IBM, Eastman Kodak, Digital Equipment, Wang, Unisys, Hewlett-Packard, NCR, and LaserData, all of which appear to be in the market for keeps. In its first full year of operation in this field, IBM reached sales of $300 million.

Interestingly, FileNet's equipment and systems worked so well that some vendors had them manufacture optical disk library hardware to their specifica-tions. Others developed software based on the FileNet model (called WorkFlo). However, this is not copyright infringement. Most installations share many common features, so software packages of necessity will bear

Fig. 1-2. The FileNet Corporation, founded by Ted Smith, at the left in the photograph, was the first successful commercial venture in image processing in the United States. Also shown (from left to right) are Robert C. Reece (manufacturing), Edward A. Miller (engineering), Lawrence S. Jordan (sales), David C. Seigle (marketing), and Mark S. St.Clare (finance). Since this picture was taken, some of the responsibilities were realigned and two more officers added. (Courtesy FileNet)

strong resemblances. This example is no different than the obvious resemblances among today's popular word processors.

Of this flood of new installations, perhaps the best known (certainly the most described in the literature) is USAA in San Antonio, Texas. USAA is a diversified insurance and financial institution serving approximately two million members, primarily officers and former officers of the armed services. Its chairman, retired Air Force Brigadier General Robert F. McDermott, set forth the goal of a paperless office environment in January 1969. By 1987, two experimental prototypes convinced USAA that it was on the right track. Accordingly, USAA asked nine companies to bid on what would then be the largest image-processing installation. Moreover, USAA insisted that what was bid either was, or would become, a standard product. IBM rose to that challenge, won the contract, and in the process nudged image technology from the sidelines into the mainstream. See B-1 for more detail.*

IBM's approach, called *ImagePlus*, can use existing mainframes or minis for the host computer. The workstations are standard PS/2 microcomputers modified with several boards to accommodate image-processing needs. Scanners, printers, and other hardware, are, for the most part, purchased from other manufacturers. The optical disk libraries were made by FileNet to IBM's specifications, though IBM has demonstrated its own library technology. It is widely rumored that IBM will eventually build an optical disk library.

Other major vendors took a somewhat different approach. For example, Eastman Kodak focuses on leveraging its traditional strengths of image capture, storage management, software, and printer output and went so far as to outsource its internal data processing operations to IBM. Its systems are designed to work on almost any computer and also integrate microform technology into systems for those customers who continue to rely on that medium. Digital Equipment Corporation (DEC), on the other hand, does not make optical disk libraries and so markets systems in a working partnership with Kodak (and others). By contrast, Unisys markets a more complete system under its own name, but continues to license elements of it from FileNet and other vendors.

1.2 Primary advantages and some disadvantages

Image processing offers many advantages, although not every installation benefits from each one. Most of these advantages translate into financial leverage directly or indirectly. Although it is true that the writers who catalogue the advantages produce different lists, those differences tend to be generalized alloys of precise descriptions.

---

*References to generic models (Appendix A), cases examples (Appendix B), and technical notes (Appendix C), are always cited by using the appendix letter plus the numbered section within the appendix.

- **Direct cost savings.** Virtually all installations free storage space, and in most cases, permit a reduction in the work force. These advantages are somewhat offset by the higher skill levels required for the personnel who operate the system, and by the space required for existing documents in some installations. Still, the savings are usually large enough to pay back the up-front costs in a period from less than one year to no more than three years.

- **Improved productivity.** Most installations improve productivity as a result of the obvious mechanical features of an image processing system. As described later, these features offer startling improvements compared to manual records management.

- **Competitive edge.** Vendors universally argue that the strategic advantage of image systems is their ability to respond to customer and potential customer inquiries instantly, rather than in days or weeks. This capability, the claim says, cannot fail to help any corporation improve profits or increase its share of the marketplace or both. As a very minimum, the claim continues, the system will improve customer satisfaction and therefore shore up the existing market base. In practice, many corporations and government agencies have justified the purchase of an image system almost solely on this capability.

  Unfortunately, this aspect is hard to measure and prove, a point examined in more detail in section 1.6.

At least four mechanical features of image processing contribute to these advantages:

- **Fast retrieval.** What formerly took hours, days, or weeks, now takes seconds at best or minutes at worst. True, an image is not a hardcopy document, but hardcopy can be printed at most workstations in seconds. Interestingly, some corporations place obstacles between workers and printers to reduce paper copies.

- **Concurrent access.** If data processing records are paralleled, any image record can be accessed by any number of simultaneous users, unless the organization makes a point of preventing it. This system eliminates routing documents, unless the processing must follow a definite sequence. That is, when each processing step depends on previous steps, the concurrent access is not a benefit for processing (although it remains an advantage for subsequent access).

- **Processing and distribution control.** The automation of document records also means that processing can be automated and controlled more efficiently than in manual systems. Here, database management systems and other software come into play. As with data processing, image processing often precipitates the elimination of unnecessary processing steps.

- **Fewer lost documents.** Once recorded, a document cannot be lost unless the optical disk on which it is stored is lost, destroyed, or if the indexing system is destroyed. Many security measures reduce these risks, as discussed in chapter 10. Short of a rare errant disk, documents simply are not lost, even when managers try to "lose" them to test the system.

Now the negatives. The up-front costs are usually high, and many new vendors in the field have not had sufficient time to build solid reputations. Moreover, the rapid expansion pace has created a shortage of experts, which means that some vendors are not capable of satisfying customer needs. Concurrently, many potential customers lack the insight and experience to know what to ask for. Some observers suggest this lack of expertise is more severe than is commonly acknowledged.

Other problems include the acceptability of image document copies as evidence in legal settings and a lack of industry-wide standards, although AIIM has made great strides in the former arena. Still other problems emanate from conditions unique to each installation, such as incompatibility with present data processing systems, networks, and a host of other specifics. Part III of this book addresses many of these issues. Some problems are overrated; others are serious. No problem cannot be conquered, but in some cases, the potential solutions could negate the advantages. Finally, a few executives abhor any automated systems form and will go to great lengths to avoid using them. If your boss is one of these types, nothing will help.

1.3 Generic configuration and open architecture

The term *image processing* is somewhat misleading for many current installations. Image databasing would be more accurate. That is, most of the processing composes routine acquisition and index/linking of records for future access. Further, as mentioned above, most documents that are generated by an image system consist of text files superimposed over a standard form image (recorded only once in the database). So most installations are variations of a generic application. The variations described in Appendix A are all based on this common model, illustrated in FIG. 1-3.

The significance of this commonality is that vendors have opted for a so-called "open architectural approach." This means, in theory, that the components of image processing are interchangeable. It doesn't work this way in practice, but the ability to mix and match various elements from different vendors is marked compared to those in data processing systems, even in the

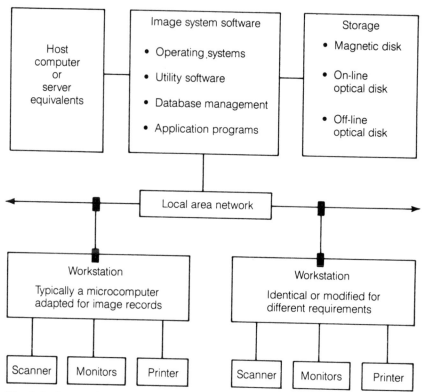

Fig. 1-3. A generic image-processing configuration. Most image system installations consist of a number of workstations networked to an optical disk drive library unit, powered either by a host computer or server units similar to data processing workstations.

absence of industry-wide standards. Many explanations have been proffered of how this came to pass, but most are related to the simplicity of the generic configuration and its components.

- **Workstations.** Image processing workstations differ little from their data processing equivalents. The principal visible difference, at least for stations used to acquire documents, is a scanner. The second difference would be the presence of larger monitors to accommodate the larger images, although ordinary VGA/EGA monitors can be used in a pinch. Otherwise, the typical equipment is a desktop computer, keyboard, and perhaps a printer. The image-record hardware usually consists of cards that can be installed in desktop computers. However, it should be noted that some systems employ larger consoles that can have built-in servers, small optical disk drives, microform readers, or any number of other components common to image processing.

- **Storage/memory.** The vast majority of image records are stored on optical disks, most of which are 12 inches in diameter. Online access is via an optical disk library, commonly called a *jukebox* because it works almost exactly like those old machines did. Less frequently accessed records are kept on the shelf and are inserted manually, and intensely accessed images are often stored magnetically.

- **Central processors or servers.** Some systems are supported by central processors, others by servers, similar to some existing workstation networks. The former need little modification to support image processing, and the latter can accommodate data processing.

- **Networks.** For local area networks, token rings and Ethernets are the most popular means, and these again require very little modification. For distribution, existing wide-area networks suffice; however, the time required to transmit much longer records is a major factor to consider.

- **Software.** Software for routine image acquisition, indexing, and access has been all but perfected, and most of it will easily link with applications software to meet unique requirements.

This building block approach suggests that the challenge of open architecture is easy to meet. Unfortunately, in the absence of standardization, it is not easy across the board. The one item that is nearly standard is the algorithm used to compress an image record (described in technical note C.3). This algorithm (actually there are several minor variations) compresses text-based document images by a factor between 10 and 15, the same one used in FAX machines. Thus scanners and printers are often as interchangeable as pieces in a TinkerToy® set.

It goes downhill from there. True, any component can be made to fit into any system, but sometimes only at the price of expensive emulation hardware and software. So the question becomes: how much open architecture can you afford? The answer to that question is different for vendors than for customers, and for the latter it also depends on the equipment on hand or the personal preferences. Moreover, once an organization opts for a specific image-processing system, major architectural changes are more expensive than upgrading from, say, ABC software version 3.7 to version 3.8. If it means a change of vendors, a great deal of so-called institutional knowledge can be lost in the process.

Figure 1-4 illustrates the situation. The culprit is the length of documents that must be imaged. If an ordinary 8½-by-11-inch document must be stored at 200 dots per inch in both dimensions (467,500 bytes of information) or roughly 155 times the length of a record that stored only the text recorded on that same document, then it must be reduced by algorithm, which fortunately adheres to an existing standard. But once reduced, it still must be stored. What size disk will be used? What is the format of that disk? What physical or

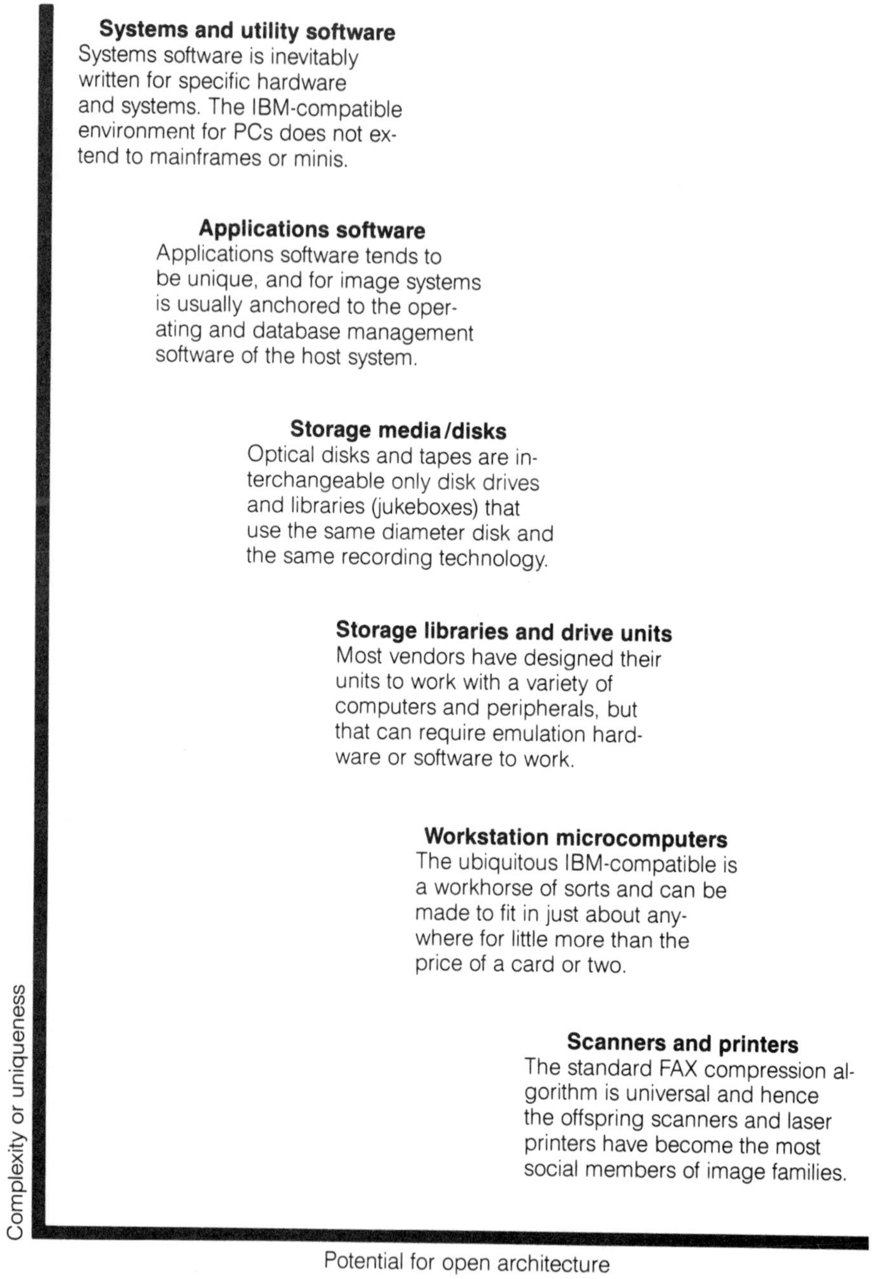

Systems and utility software
Systems software is inevitably
written for specific hardware
and systems. The IBM-compatible
environment for PCs does not ex-
tend to mainframes or minis.

Applications software
Applications software tends to
be unique, and for image systems
is usually anchored to the operating and database management
software of the host system.

Storage media/disks
Optical disks and tapes are interchangeable only disk drives
and libraries (jukeboxes) that
use the same diameter disk and
the same recording technology.

Storage libraries and drive units
Most vendors have designed their
units to work with a variety of
computers and peripherals, but
that can require emulation hardware or software to work.

Workstation microcomputers
The ubiquitous IBM-compatible is
a workhorse of sorts and can be
made to fit in just about anywhere for little more than the
price of a card or two.

Scanners and printers
The standard FAX compression algorithm is universal and hence
the offspring scanners and laser
printers have become the most
social members of image families.

Complexity or uniqueness

Potential for open architecture

*Fig. 1-4. Open and not-so-open architecture. Different components of image sys-
tems manufactured by different vendors work together remarkably well. But the
opportunities are not infinite, at least not without counterproductive emulations.*

chemical process is used to etch the surface to record the information? What index logic will be used, on what software, operating on what computer? How is this document linked to related documents? How long must they be kept? Are related records reconsolidated on other disks?

At this point, the reader could ask, "Just how open is open architecture?" The answer resides in how vendors capitalize on those opportunities that require the least expensive or the least-disabling emulation to make the pieces work together well. IBM can afford to design its systems to work only on IBM computers for the simple reason that the majority of mainframes (and a healthy slice of the minis) in existence are made by IBM. However, although IBM makes scanners, it relies primarily on those made by other vendors. Those other vendors have more experience building scanners and they have few interface problems.

1.4 Levels of application

The generic configuration applies to all organizational levels, but the details rise in complexity for the same reason that the dispatch of a fleet of moving vans is more complex than managing a single-van delivery service. However, hardware and communications are seldom the problem. On the contrary, many of the first successful installations took higher levels into account. However, the difficulty arises with document linkage and relating an increasing amount of diverse data and records, and also with controlling the processing of similar or related documents. These difficulties are little different than those that occur in data processing. As outlined in FIG. 1-5, the levels are:

- **Functional level.** At this level, the image system has a singular, well-defined scope and purpose, and is usually operated by a handful of personnel. An example would be a standalone file of reference material that could range in size from a few hundred to several million documents, perhaps more. On a scale of 1 to 100, the difficulty of installing a system at this level is seldom higher than 10. On the other hand, the potential savings per dollar invested are likely to be less than for more complex installations.

- **Departmental level.** At this level, the scope is still singular, but the operations are more diversified. For example, insurance processing requires a variety of processing for higher complexity, despite that the variety of documents might be less than for a functional level. On the 1-to-100 scale, difficulty of installation can range from 10 to perhaps as high as 60, although as the number of installations increase, the experience lowers the difficulty.

• **Enterprise level.** At this level, all documentation image systems in a corporation or in its organizational equivalent are integrated: for example, all internal banking operations. However, the scope could also cover all operations of a diversified multinational company. Understandably then, the complexity of installing a system of this nature can range from 30 to 100 on the scale of difficulty. Moreover, the return on investment of attempting to integrate information and documents in highly diversified operations is not always as high as planned. In some cases, therefore, a better approach could be to use independent departmental-level operations as necessary, with linkage only where needed.

	Scope of activity	Requirements and problems
Functional level	• Singular, well-defined purpose; often unrelated to other functions • Usually in support of a small group of individuals	• From 1 to 10 workstations, powered by a minicomputer • Not always as cost effective in proportion to larger systems
Department level	• Singular activity that is broader in scope • Often marked by an intense number of acquisitions and accesses	• One or more networks of workstations, often powered by a mainframe • Hundreds of details are often overlooked during planning
Enterprise level	• Covers every aspect of an organization that relies heavily on documentation • Can be narrowly or widely focused	• Can be any size, but more often than not a series of departmental-level setups • Integration of componets can be difficult

Fig. 1-5. Organizational levels of use. Image systems work the same at all organizational levels, much more so than conventional processing, but the technical differences are critical and must be built into lower-level systems to support the integrations that are intended for higher levels.

The ability to distribute copies of imaged documents worldwide should not be confused with various application levels. A functional level system could be housed in one room and still be accessed anywhere in the world via a communications network. Conversely, an enterprise-level system could operate in hundreds of different locations with little traffic among them. In short, network technology can accommodate just about any transmission requirement, although it could prove to be expensive. The complexity resides in variety of documents recorded, the linkage of related documents, and the amount of processing required. The dividing lines between the three levels are not always orderly, but the idea is clear.

1.5 The cost picture

Vendors will quote prices for components, but are reluctant to do so for entire systems. One reason is to avoid discouraging customers with the unavoidably high up-front costs before the vendor has a chance to outline the return on the investment. More importantly, too many variables exist at each installation to warrant any kind of useful over-the-counter estimates. However, as graphed in FIG. 1-6, several ballpark figures are available, and the decision support spreadsheet program, included in Appendix D, has been designed to let each user enter actual costs. Thus, with such-and-such set of prices and operating costs, the total cost would be so-and-so, and the return on investment thus-and-thus. Change the numbers, and different answers are returned. The ballpark figures are:

- Functional Level $30 thousand to $200 thousand
- Departmental Level $300 thousand to $1 million
- Enterprise Level $1 million to don't even think about it

One vendor said that a 40-workstation department-level system costs about $600 thousand plus 25 to 50 percent for consulting and meeting unique requirements. However, many installations have or plan to have more than one thousand terminals, and when it comes to the system planned for the Internal Revenue Service, the total cost will undoubtedly be billions. Many other projects, especially those for other federal agencies, will also come with high price tags.

Still, the issue is not the up-front cost, but the return on investment. How much space will be freed, and what is its value? Can the space be used for other purposes? If it is owned and not needed, can it be sold? If it is leased, can the lease be broken? How much of a net staffing reduction is in the offering? Are there union contracts that will make reduction difficult, or does the company have policy of reduction by attrition only? Will current documentation be maintained in paper form until it can be destroyed legally, and if so, what are the offsetting expenses for maintaining a dual system—at least for the transition period?

Cost analysis for image processing systems is anything but sure and simple. Moreover, many corporate executives admit that they purchased a system without a detailed cost analysis. The deciding factor in these cases was the strategic advantage or to meet some other requirement. They assume that in the long run, image processing will cost less than continuing with manual procedures.

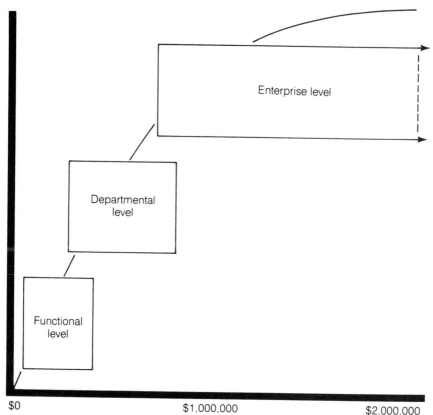

Fig. 1-6. Cost ranges. Costs vary with level, and within each level, the uniqueness of each installation negates the utility of ballpark figures. Each corporation should prepare its own analysis, unless it is convinced that the subjective advantages outweigh any possible cost increase.

Added to this confusion are the unknowns of future expansions and enhancements, and the even more subjective issues that are associated with changing the organization to react to the advantages afforded by image processing. It is well-known that only about one or two percent of organizational information is available in automated on-line form, and perhaps another four percent is in microform or semi-automated off-line storage. When image processing is used to the hilt, however, the percentage can rise to 100 percent in theory and perhaps as high as 90 percent in practice. That order of magnitude can and should dictate major changes to the way any organization conducts its business, and perhaps to the scope of its business and influence.

1.6 The strategic-advantage argument

As previously stated, every vendor touts image processing for the strategic advantages it provides, as well as for the potential return on investment. The reasoning goes that if one company can respond to a customer much faster than the competition, it is bound to increase its market share of the business. In the case of nonprofit operations, the idea of improving services for the same dollar amount has equal appeal.

As soon as each competitor begins to lose market position, he is likely to adapt the same technology in order to regain the position. Thus, in time, the marketplace will return to the state it was in before the introduction of the technology. Then vendors will offer the next strategic advantage.

It is true that under exceptional conditions, a new technology can push a corporation into a commanding lead in the marketplace that will not likely suffer in the foreseeable future. Unfortunately, this phenomena tends to apply to vendors more than to customers, witness xerography. The open architectural environment of image processing could negate even that potential. So, several points need to be considered before a decisionmaker bases his or her conclusion on the subjective nature of strategic advantage:

- **Difficulty of confirming the advantage.** It is nearly impossible to attribute an increase of market share or even to retain what exists to image processing. Too many other factors operate in the marketplace, and thus it is almost impossible to measure the impact of imaging.

- **Fast service isn't everything.** Rapid response to customer inquiries doesn't always translate to increased market share. If the personnel are rude or offensive, it could accelerate decline.

- **Don't underestimate the competition.** Even if competitors are slow to adopt image processing, they will likely use other means of improving their own market position. That is, imaging is very exciting to those who are convinced of its utility, but alternative approaches for improving productivity excite others.

In short, image processing offers undeniable advantages to nearly every type of corporation or organization, but it is not a panacea.

1.7 Emergence of the information engineer

The computer age has spawned many new job titles. Two of the more intriguing ones are chief information officer (CIO) and systems engineer. Image processing will undoubtedly add to the list; arguably, the most fascinating of these new titles will be information engineer or its equivalent. The title will bridge the gap between the CIO and the systems engineer.

The basis for this is the change from a tiny fraction of an organization's information being available in automated or semi-automated form to a majority (possibly an overwhelming majority) that permits instant access and processing. The task of linking this information in a useful, as well as a technically efficient, manner suggests that the CIO should become more technically oriented, or conversely, the systems engineer should become more cognizant of organizational priorities.

These changes might not happen. Instead, the best of the records management personnel and the more broadly educated of the information systems staff could gravitate to meet this challenge. A recent issue of *Forbes* magazine (November 26, 1990) went so far as to make this concern a cover story. *Forbes* said that image processing will expand the computer market explosively in the next decade, and sales are projected at $35 billion by the turn of the century. Some analysts project higher figures than this because the direct cost savings will motivate most corporations to adopt this technology.

Ambitious young managers will also see that this could become a new route to top management, primarily as a result of the increasing emphasis on success as a function of processing information inexpensively. It follows that graduate business schools will begin to offer courses in the narrower field of image processing and to increase emphasis on courses on automated information management. Where it will all end is anybody's guess, but the end is nowhere in sight.

2

Theoretical factors

It's always something.

Gilda Radner

Few managers have much patience for theory, and the metaphysical insanities concocted in physics in this century suggest that a number of scientists don't appreciate its discipline either. Nevertheless, image processing comes packaged with a number of theoretical factors that determine the financial success of an installation or at least offer a perspective from which to evaluate its feasibility for imaging.

The first of these composes the polemics of images. At one end are images from which data can be extracted or at least linked to other data. At the other end are sets of data, from which images can be generated. The second factor is a composite of pyramids and hierarchies that are common to all sciences. For image systems, "the pyramid" refers to perspective and "the hierarchy" to utility.

Next, the concept of *power curve* is a variation on the idea of diminishing returns. For image processing, it means, for example, that too small a system will not yield a positive return on investment, and an excessive investment will yield marginal returns at best and perhaps reduce prior savings. Closely related to this concept, the theory of *interior lines* is the degree to which a system can assemble diverse information rapidly at low cost to meet one or more objectives or requirements. These factors support a list of parameters that influence the success or failure of an image system. Some have become academic; others persist.

2.1 Polemics

For all its outward simplicity, image processing operates with an intricate array of factors. Part of this intricacy arises from the inherent polemics of image processing. By contrast, data processing is not faced with this problem. The latter starts with data, does something with it, and ends up with different data. The differences between *character data*, which is stored symbol by symbol, and numerical data, which is often stored and is always computed in binary form, are of little significance at any perspective higher than a programmer's. But image processing is different. An image is something that can only be interpreted by human vision, unless two images are compared for differences or if part of one image is compared with a standard.

Next, the polemics of images must be addressed, as shown in FIG. 2-1. Is the image captured as an image, and then linked with digital data (or in some cases, usually by way of optical character recognition, converted to processable data)? This *raster image* is captured bit by bit, and the equivalent of the raster image is formed on an ordinary television screen or monitor.

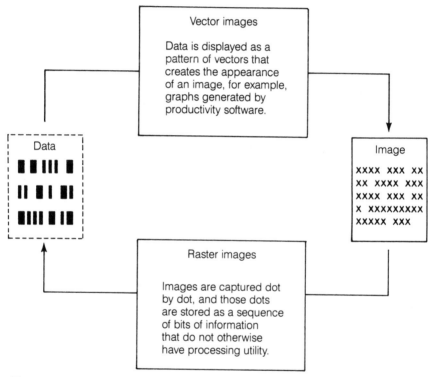

Fig. 2-1. Documents are either acquired bit-by-bit as a raster image, or generated from data as a vector image. The two types are merged when a raster image is converted to text by OCR technology, and then redisplayed as a vector image. The payoff is reduced costs.

Or will the image be generated from processable data? Graphs created by productivity software are a good example of this polemic, *the vector*, though many scientific applications are a hundred times more sophisticated. A vector is an arrow with direction—in practical terms, it is the data that instructs a monitor to display a line of points of "such-and-such length, beginning at so-

and-so point, in thus-and-thus direction." Complex generated images are always composites of vectors, although for a curved line, each vector only needs to be one-point long. The scientific term for this concept is *loci*.

Many vendors argue that image systems are intended to capture documents "as is," to which users add indexing data and any other information necessary to retrieve and use the records. This argument is true in the simplest models, but many installations generate documents that are vector images—text files printed or displayed on forms. In this case, each letter or symbol is the equivalent of a vector. Also note that the long-range potential for optical character recognition means that raster images will eventually be replaced by vector images, which in turn will permit a major reduction in storage requirements.

As mentioned at the beginning of this section, aside from a few scientific and intelligence activities, a pure image cannot be processed, except in the limited sense of using an algorithm to reduce the record length. It doesn't matter if the image is acquired as an image or generated from data; once formed, its utility accrues almost solely to the ability of the individual who uses it. In other words, it must be the right image, at the right place, at the right time, with sufficient resolution to make all relevant detail clear, and it must usually be available in conjunction with related documents or other images. So, in image processing, the human interface with the computer is far more important than it is with data processing. Many more individuals without experience or education in computer science will likely have to use the system directly.

2.2 Pyramids and hierarchies

From an aircraft in flight, the ground usually appears peaceful and serene, even in foul weather. Then as the plane approaches the runway, the foul weather becomes more apparent. Next, after missing a critical connection, the traveler becomes upset. After arriving at the destination, he or she discovers that the luggage has been lost; and the attitude degenerates into hostility. This example sometimes represents managerial perspectives that emanate from different levels.

In brief, management often looks at projects from four levels. At each lower level, the number of incumbents increases from the previous level by a factor of ten, and arguably the level of detail increases by a similar factor. A single detail rarely defeats a system, but in their mass, these details can cause more damage than a dozen bulldozers.

- **The strategic level.** Incumbents at the strategic level in most corporations rarely include more than two or three key decisionmakers (sometimes just one) who are responsible for the organization; therefore their decisions have ramifications for years to come. This level will likely decide whether or not to acquire a major image-processing system, and if acquired, they will decide what it should be expected to do. If that decision is made without considering the mass of underlying detail, the lower levels will suffer accordingly.

- **The operational level.** For every strategic-level decisionmaker, 10 operational-level executives exist. They implement decisions and make an organization work from month to month. Successful installations can usually be traced to successful incumbents at this level.

- **The managerial/supervisory/foreman level.** At this level, the ratio increases another tenfold to 100. These individuals will make an image system work from day to day, and will note the progress and problems of individual workers.

- **The worker level.** The lowest level of perspective, of course, is comprised of the workers who, by the nature of their work tend to make many informal decisions, and will likely reach one thousand or more (sometimes many more) for every strategic-level decisionmaker. Image systems reduce some of the workers, but more skills are required from those who remain.

Synergistic rung	At this level, the system generates benefits beyond its intended return on investment. Difficult to achieve.
Productive rung	At the productive-level, all goals are fulfilled and the system yields a solid return on investment.
Passable rung	At the passable-rung level, an image system meets requirements without a significant return on investment.
Sputtering rung	A sputtering-rung system is intended to meet requirements but it is so ill-designed that it usually fails.
Survival rung	At this level, the system satisfies the whims of a misguided executive without supporting real requirements.

Fig. 2-2. The hierarchy of image systems utility. All systems vary in utility, from those installed to satisfy a misguided decision to those that return information worth the proverbial weight in gold. But the highest level is not always practical for routine-transaction systems.

Turning next to the concept of hierarchies, image processing has one that is a counterpart to its data-processing cousin. This hierarchy is a paraphrase of the one developed by Abraham Maslow to illustrate needs in human psychology, shown in FIG. 2-2. However, reaching for the highest level can be counterproductive. Transaction-based systems develop utility from the efficient processing of routine work. Information gleaned from composite data might or might not contribute to higher corporate objectives, except in the limited sense of monitoring the system itself. And image systems tend to lend themselves to this highest level less than their data-processing counterparts do. Case B.2 (Northwest Airlines) is an exception to the rule.

2.3 The power curve

The *power curve* describes system efficiency. A system continues to sputter until a certain level of volume, or alternatively, a critical arrangement or configuration is reached. After that point, efficiency improves markedly with only marginal additions or improvements, until another level is reached. After that point, the return on investment falls rapidly and perhaps reaches a point of negative returns. As illustrated in FIG. 2-3, the power curve permeates image processing. Its significance to management is that too little or too much can defeat the goals of an image system, although the shape of it varies with the installation. A few examples follow:

- **History of image technology.** Image technology began in the 1920s and moved along at a nearly imperceptible pace until about 1970. At that point, the curve began to shift slowly upward until 1985 when the commercial applications first became successful. From that time forward, the power curve section began and will probably continue until most organizations that can benefit from an installation will already have them. After that, return on investment will likely drop.

- **Investment level.** Small prototypes seldom demonstrate the effectiveness of image processing. Not until it takes over the records management functions of an entire department, frees the old storage space, and reduces the staff costs, will this happen. After that point is reached, the attempt to push the technology into every nook and cranny of an organization could prove to be uneconomical.

- **Documents included in a system.** An image system will demonstrate its mettle only after a sufficient number of documents are included. After that point, the return on investment continues unabated until the volume no longer justifies the cost. For example, the law firm of Ernest & Young states that for a complex case, hundreds of thousands of documents might be checked, but only 500 of those will be relevant. For this type of system, the optimum setup would store only the more important references on-line, and the balance on the shelf.

• **Speed of document retrieval.** Above the inherent design levels, improved access speed can increase costs at an exponential rate. This rate will quickly diminish returns.

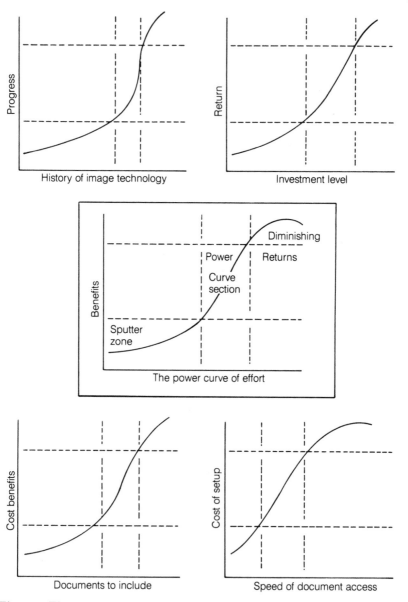

Fig. 2-3. The power curve is a derivative of normal distribution and the point of diminishing returns. It applies to image systems in several of ways, including the amount of documentation that must be included before it begins to pay for itself.

2.4 Interior lines

The term *interior lines* connotes the ability to shift resources of any kind to meet any requirement or objective, without encountering significant hindrance or difficulty. In terms of records management, good interior lines translate to an efficient organization and a comprehensive, but simple logic for filing documents—ideally in the same general location. Then, regardless of what documentation is needed to meet a requirement, the necessary records can be retrieved and compiled as appropriate at the mere touch of a finger. It's a wonderful concept, but few, if any, organizations have been able to approach it. On the contrary, many people have trouble finding a letter in their desk drawer, and a file cabinet presents an even greater obstacle.

Napoleon dealt with this common problem in an unusual way. He threw all correspondence in a drawer and ignored it. His reasoning was that 90 percent of the problems raised would dissipate in three weeks. Of the remainder, Napoleon believed that the writers were sure to visit him for an answer. Unfortunately, this approach does not work for insurance claims, applications for loans or driver licenses, for building permits, or any of the other hundreds of transactions that support business and personal life. The reason is that the vast majority of those transactions must be addressed in conjunction with other documents. The ability to assemble documents quickly is the essence of interior lines. Image processing offers this capability in spades, though any form of automated system can do the same.

Consider, for example, the differences between Lotus 1-2-3 versions 2.2 and 3.1, and the capability of Microsoft Windows 3.0. In the case of Lotus 1-2-3, version 2.2 offers desktop publishing capabilities by way of an adjunct piece of software, Allways. The problem is that the user must shift back and forth between Lotus and Allways in order to make changes to the data on a spreadsheet while formatting it for presentation. Version 3.1 better integrates these two functions into one system, redesigning the interior lines of the software (noting that the new version also adds additional formatting features). In the case of Windows, the user can jump among several software packages, concurrently booted, and transfer parts of files among them, including automated file reformatting for software packages designed to work with it.

In short, interior lines are an inexpensive means of improving investment returns for a given amount of hardware and software. For image systems, the prime source of efficient interior lines arise from the use of relational database logic to create the index and add attributes to the records. In a relational data base, all records are treated equally and therefore any that pertain to a specific case can be readily assembled, provided that the necessary information is recorded in the index and that a sound logic underwrites the various codes for documents. Some image systems create electronic folders in which routinely related documents are automatically assembled into one "file folder." These points are described at greater length in chapter 5 and in technical note, C.5.

that the bulk of processing consists of recording and retrieving images to support manual processing and decisionmaking. Above that level, the goal is to transform or translate information into intelligence.

Defining or even describing this metamorphosis is difficult, but most definitions of intelligence state that it occurs when pieces of information are brought together so that they support the potential for decisionmaking that could not otherwise occur. That is, information composes facts and data, whereas intelligence seeks interpretation of, trends from, interrelations among, insights from, and understandings of that information. For image-processing systems, this occurs in two forms:

- **Direct perception.** *Direct perception* occurs when a user can support decisionmaking by the ability to view related documents concurrently. Image processing, per se, does not support this process in a direct sense. The user could just as easily view the related documents on paper. The time it takes to gather these documents, however, would discourage one to do so. Thus, an image system encourages this level of intelligence indirectly.

- **Automated intelligence.** *Automated intelligence* is a system that can perform interpretations of information. Optical character recognition is a low-level application of this form; complex engineering drawings comparison is a higher level application.

The significance for managers is that a system will climb the rungs of the utility hierarchy to the extent that its interior lines afford it. In a sense, then, it all boils down to how much clerical work is automated and how fast that automation operates, short of diminishing the investment return.

2.5 Parameters

The theoretical considerations, especially interior lines, yield at least 18 factors that impact the profitability and utility of image-processing systems. Some can be taken for granted (at least for large installations), others demand careful evaluation and planning. If a project seems to be waving red flags on one or more factors, then it should be reconsidered. Figure 2-4 illustrates the relationships among these factors. Of them, the four data base-oriented basic factors are:

- **Acquirability.** *Acquirability*, or *acquisition*, refers to the process by which paperwork or other input is reduced to an electronic image and then indexed for subsequent retrieval. Every image in an image database must be acquired, but this process is often the most expensive operational cost of the system and is a frequent source of errors and bottlenecks.

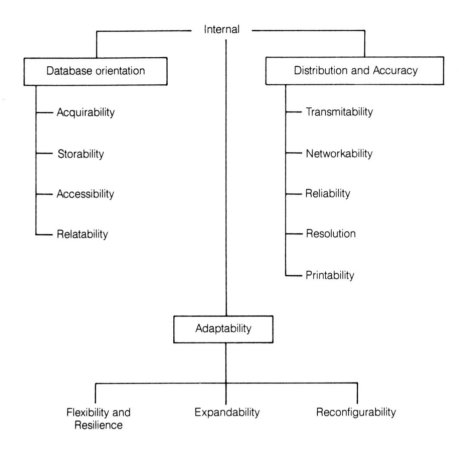

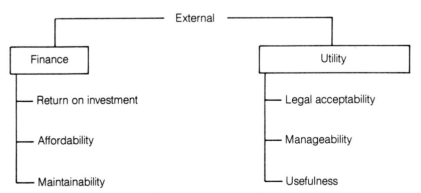

Fig. 2-4. Image processing offers clear opportunities for major cost savings, and perhaps to gain a temporary strategic advantage. Yet irrespective of the numbers, a wide range of factors must coalesce to make the system work well.

- **Storability.** Image records must be stored, usually on magnetic media (if instant access is required) and on optical disks (if minor delays in access can be tolerated). Unfortunately, on-line magnetic storage is more expensive than its optical counterpart and if relied on exclusively, would soon overtax the host computer's ability to handle its peripherals. The optical disk library saves the day, providing that a substantial number of records can be stored off-line after a period of time in on-line status. This factor is rarely a problem anymore.

- **Accessibility.** *Accessibility* is related to storability. Any record that is stored can be retrieved, but time and adequate indexing are critical.

- **Reliability.** *Reliability* is the ability to logically and electronically relate image records with themselves and other data. This can be accomplished by coding the images to be accessed or by logically relating the text data and images.

The next five factors cover transmission and quality of access:

- **Transmitability.** The retrieval of an image record on a terminal clearly demonstrates its *transmitability*, but the issue here addresses the cost and time required to transmit image traffic over sizable distances, if necessary.

- **Networkability.** Networks are *de rigueur* for image processing in all but a few small systems. In theory, any network can support any image processing system that has terminals in the necessary locations, but only a few actually can support it well.

- **Reliability.** *Reliability* is the degree to which a bit stream at the point of reception matches what is sent at the point of transmission. This applies to image processing as well as to digital data. Fortunately, most image records are more tolerant of minor discrepancies here, because the viewer can usually decipher the altered image, and typically, only a small fraction of the record is critical.

- **Readability.** *Readability* refers primarily to image or screen resolution. The more precise and small the detail, the more memory each image will require. This memory, in turn, can mean the difference between a mainframe setup and a mini.

- **Printability.** Except as restricted by copyright laws, any document that can be read can be printed. The catch is that image processing is intended to reduce paperwork. The more printing that is required, the more the objectives of the system could be compromised.

The next three factors cover the ability of a system to adapt to changing requirements. This problem is somewhat more complex than for conventional processing, both for reasons of technology and because it is more difficult to envision all the potential of a new field.

- **Flexibility and resilience.** These attributes measure the capability of a system to adapt readily to changing loads and requirements. The means to flexibility can vary from the ability to distribute peak loads among other workstations to the capability of dealing with a wide range of document types.

- **Expandability.** *Expandability* is the capability of a system to accept greater loads by adding a minimum of hardware. The problem is fundamentally no different than in conventional processing, but the technology poses unique questions. As such, expansion plans can incur greater difficulties than the original installation.

- **Reconfigurability.** *Reconfigurability* is closely related to expandability; here, the emphasis is on the ability to rearrange existing components to meet the unexpected by permanently changing the requirements—a side benefit of open architectural design.

The next three factors concern finance:

- **Return on investment.** An image processing system can pay for itself in two ways: by reducing the net cost of acquiring and maintaining records and other documentation, and by strategic or competitive advantage, at least until the competition adopts the same strategy. The first is easy to pin down. The second, as discussed in section 1.6, is somewhat ephemeral and depends on a host of subjective factors. When betting heavily on the second source at the expense of the first, the system might work well in the procedural sense, but there is no assurance that it will pay for itself.

- **Affordability.** An image system in most instances is an expensive investment and cost savings are sometimes overestimated. More to the point and irrespective of long-term benefits, it must be funded. Worse, small-scale implementations rarely pay for themselves—unless a self-contained desktop microcomputer setup can be used.

- **Maintainability.** *Maintainability* usually connotes maintenance, but the latter is hardly a financial factor, except in the limited sense of costs. In this field, maintainability is the ability to keep a system running at an affordable cost. Repeated breakdowns or the need to continually modify software in the absence of major changes to requirements exemplify this factor. The equivalent in automobile manufacture is the so-called lemon.

The last three factors address the use of the system itself. They are more varied and more troublesome than any of the previous categories.

- **Legal sustainability.** If image documents are required to support legal proceedings, or at least reveal the potential for this need, but the courts will accept only original documentation (or a less electronic substitute such as microfilm), the opportunity to dispose of the original paperwork is negated. However, a less expensive means of storage could be found.

- **Manageability.** As systems grow large, they can become unmanageable. This has not been the case with systems installed to date, but as they grow in complexity, the risk increases.

- **Usability.** A system that runs well in the mechanical sense but has little practical value is worse than none at all. An impractical system drains resources.

3

Applied factors

Heights charm us, the paths
which lead to them do not.

Adolphus W. Greely

The theories presented in the previous chapter lead to many applied factors. The first is a *requirements analysis*, which determines exactly what you want an image system to do. The second factor is *loading*, the delineation of the types and magnitudes of the stored records and the changing access requirements. The third factor addresses processing and any output requirements beyond access on monitors. The fourth factor is a conglomerate that covers constraints; for example, the need to integrate the image system with other systems or to satellite it on existing hardware. The first three are common to all systems; the fourth is not.

Admittedly, this type of analysis is drudgery, but shortchanging it will inevitably result in a system that is too large or too small. Worse yet, the system might not meet requirements. According to some vendors, this is the single most pressing problem in image processing. Many customers do not take the time to understand the opportunities and limitations of this technology. They become enamored with the obvious advantages and then turn to the vendor and say "make it work for me." Bear in mind, then, the criticality of record length and numbers. All image systems are hardware hungry and have strong tastes for large optical disk libraries and workstations. They also require more human interface than data processing systems, and a wider spectrum of personnel.

3.1 Requirements analysis

What do you want an image system to do? Save money? Improve productivity? Grab a bigger share of the market? Make customers happier, or for government agencies, less dissatisfied? When the answers are clear, will an image system fill the bill? The chances are that imaging can fulfill one or more of these goals in any corporation with gross revenues of $500 thousand or more per annum (or its equivalent in services rendered), and in some corporations below this threshold. But the extent to which goals are realized is altogether a different matter.

If the advantages of an image processing system for an organization have been concluded, and the planning will be thorough, several approaches are available. Each starts with known quantities and explicit requirements and works toward the unknown. The nature of the business usually suggests what is known and what isn't. A library has a clear idea of its database, but is not always sure of the changing requirements of its "customers," especially if an image system opens up new opportunities. By contrast, an engineering firm usually has a solid idea of the work it must perform, but is not initially concerned with the nature and scope of the resulting database.

The question of approach, then, usually boils down to a choice of: starting with the image database and working to the processing, or working with requirements, reducing them to processing, and then deducing the storage requirements. In some cases, it could be beneficial to try both routes, each headed by a different analyst, and then compare the results. If the results are similar, the battle is half won. If not, the requirements have not been thoroughly thought through.

To this the critic will respond "it just isn't that simple. The system acquisition cycle in major corporations can take one year or more, and it could take nearly that long to gather information about existing procedures to make a sound evaluation." That is true; the entire process is covered at length in Part IV and is further supported by the spreadsheet model outlined in Appendix D. Still, that is not the point. The point is to nail down what is needed, and then reduce those conclusions to concise written requirements:

- What are the goals of the proposed system?
- What is the warp and woof of the necessary image database?
- What processing is required to bridge the gap between the goals and the database?

This work entails wrestling with some of the detail, both with respect to image technology and to the way business is conducted. The former can be achieved with a few site visits to successful installations, a few weeks of reading, and perhaps requests for information from several vendors. Just become knowledgeable in the field; an expert's skill isn't necessary. To become properly educated, bring some good supervisors, systems analysts, and cost accountants into the planning process. In short, the decisionmaker needs to descend a few levels on the pyramid of perspective (described in section 2.2).

3.2 Load and storage factors

Load factors are the sum of record storage requirements, the level at which each will be stored for what length of time. This sum, in an economic sense, drives the system. It dictates how much hardware will be needed and will usually establish a range in the likely number of workstations and the scope of network requirements (FIG. 3-1). To be sure, processing requirements and constraint factors will exert a major influence on the exact numbers, but in practice most installations fall into patterns. A project that holds only 20 thousand records will not likely require one thousand workstations; however, one that consumes 100 million records will seldom operate efficiently with 10 of those workstations.

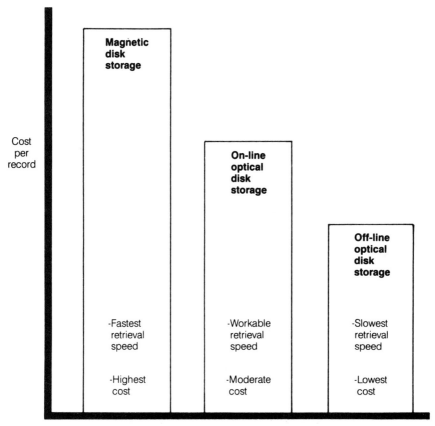

Fig. 3-1. Storage trade-offs. The fastest access times mean the highest costs. The on-line optical disk is the compromise. Magnetic storage is economical only for intense processing and low-cost off-line optical disk storage is more than sufficient for seldom accessed records.

To continue, load factors are best understood from the three common methods of storage. Not all systems use all three levels, and a few depend only on on-line optical disks.

- **Magnetic disks.** The magnetic disk drives used to store ordinary data work equally well for image systems, provided that they have the capacity to store the much longer records. In practice, they don't have this capacity, nor need they. The fast response time of these drives is necessary only for the most intense processing periods, which usually occur during the first few hours or days after a document is acquired. Thus, only a tiny fraction of the records in an image system will be stored on this medium, and some installations dispense with it entirely.

- **On-line optical disks.** Access time from optical disks is noticeably slower than from magnetic storage, ranging from one to 15 seconds. The reason is that most optical disk libraries are modeled after jukeboxes. A call for a specific record is checked against an index (which itself is almost always kept on a magnetic disk). When the optical disk on which the record is located is identified, a signal is sent to the jukebox to retrieve that disk and insert it into a driver.

- **Off-line optical disks.** This method varies from on-line storage. If the index indicates the disk is no longer on line, a message is sent to an operator who then retrieves the disk from a shelf and inserts it manually in a drive. Depending on staffing and loads, this could take anywhere from a few minutes to several hours, but the images relegated to this level of storage are rarely called for.

In one approach to the trade-off style, all records are kept on-line on optical disks and then the ideal trade-off point for moving them to off-line status is determined. This is usually measured in predictable number-of-accesses per baseline number of records per unit of time, for example, two accesses per 10 thousand records per day. Almost without exception, access requirements are lowered with the passage of time; however as shown in appendix A, the rate varies with the installation. Then, if extraordinary efficiency is required during initial processing, newly acquired records should be held in temporary magnetic storage. Notice that doubling the time doubles the tax on disk drives, and this could prove expensive.

3.3 Processing factors

Image document processing can range from simple off-the-shelf indexing software to major programming that can exceed the costs of the basic storage and retrieval part of the system. Processing can also range from data extraction from the records, to data and other document generation, to image modification, to extensive image record linking with other records. Any requirement that can be reduced to logical steps can be programmed, except those that mandate human review and decisions. Figure 3-2 illustrates the various levels of image processing software, although the dividing lines in practice are seldom that clear.

	Description	Significance
Off-the shelf	Ready to run; needs only user input to index documents. Rarely useful above functional levels.	Reduces up-front costs but limits the utility of the system. If software is to be inserted later, the indexing logic must be ready for it.
Modified off-the-shelf	Extends the ready-to-run option to departmental level installations in many cases.	Probably the most cost efficient software available, but this virtue can cause management to discount bona fide processing requirements.
Applications software	Yields exceptional flexibility for departmental-level installation. This is the norm.	Requires extensive review of existing work procedures, and can equal 50 percent or more of the hardware and other system costs.
Dominant software requirements	Almost unavoidable for enterprise-level setups, but each system will tend to be unique.	More likely than not to be integrated with existing data processing systems, and with concurrent major changes to the organization.

Fig. 3-2. Processing considerations. Software for image systems varies from off-the-shelf models to custom-built programs. To the extent that requirements intensify is the degree to which hardware issues can be downplayed. Existing technology can already meet almost any need.

- **Off-the-shelf software.** Many vendors have developed proprietary software packages that work closely with the image hardware. This software is usually adequate for acquiring, indexing, and retrieving image documents, and is something of an enhanced database management system. However, some packages also include programs for the control and management of access and updates. Few installations can meet requirements with just this level of programming, but those that do will be hardware and database-oriented.

- **Modified off-the-shelf software.** Most of the proprietary software packages have logical switches that can be set by users, or gates where relatively small user-written programs can be linked. Most installations require at least this level of processing. It is almost impossible to develop a single piece of software that can accommodate the myriad of processing requirements.

- **Applications programming.** At this level, the acquisition and access hardware becomes almost secondary to processing requirements, but processing remains highly dependent on efficient database management. The applications can range from document generation to statistical reports intended to support management of the system and the personnel operating it.

- **Dominant software requirements.** When this level is reached, the image system becomes little more than a source of input data for much larger objectives. In almost every case, the programming will be custom-developed and will have little utility beyond very similar installations. The software costs could equal the hardware costs.

The above discussion ignores issues of networking and distribution. Fortunately, local area network requirements, implied by processing and load factors, are easy to develop and install, given the experience with numerous successful installations. Most vendors consider these part of the systems they sell. Issues related to wide-area distribution are more complex and involve major trade-offs between the logical integrity offered by centralized systems and the lower communications cost of distributed systems. It is usually decided on technical grounds after requirements have been hammered out, rather than the reverse. Section 8.3 details this issue.

3.4 Constraints

Although image technology is a relatively new and sudden development, an installation will not necessarily be free of major constraints. On the contrary, most systems will have some relationship with existing data processing, however minor. Further, management could require that maximum use be made of existing hardware, which would limit the choice of vendors, despite their claims of open architecture. That is, although the products of all vendors could be made to work, the necessary emulation hardware and software would rule out many of the contenders. Finally, ceilings can exist on up-front costs, which severely limit the options a corporation can exercise. It might be shortsighted, but this situation is reality in many organizations.

The list goes on, and any attempt to describe every plausible constraint would fill a book. Every experienced manager is well aware of the range of these constraints. Still, image projects should receive special consideration. The primary reason is that at full tilt they can completely overshadow existing data processing systems, if for no other reason than by the sheer mass of records and the equally massive storage requirements. It is not an add-on feature, though many installations are powered by existing mainframes. Also notice that the processing drain on those computers is minimal; the bulk of the processing work is done by the workstation hardware.

Another point of consideration is that, as mentioned elsewhere, most installations lead to major internal reorganizations. Those reorganizations could make the constraints obsolete. This doesn't mean the task of convincing heels-dug-in decisionmakers will be any easier, but it's worth a stab.

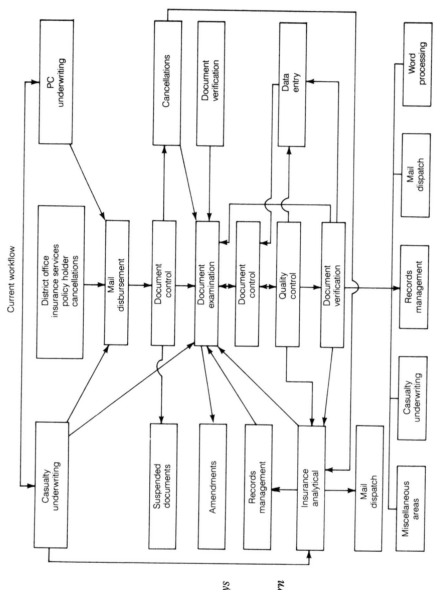

Fig. 3-3. Part of imaging productivity is inherent in the technology; the rest is a result of careful planning. The insurance division of the Automobile Club of Southern California displays these before-and-after schematics of their procedures. (Courtesy Automobile Club of Southern California)

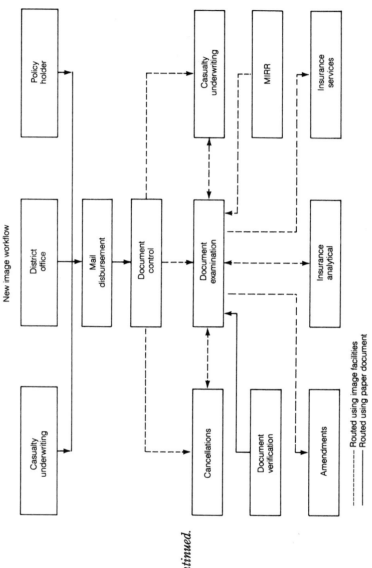

Fig. 3-3. Continued.

3.5 Tying it all together

Goals. Loads. Processing. These terms need to be integrated into a logical statement of requirements. Organizing these terms is often similar to following a road map. A good example is the insurance processing division of the Auto Club of Southern California. In the process of developing detailed requirements, management found that many existing procedures had become unnecessary—even without an image system. Other procedures were eliminated by the system. Figure 3-3 illustrates the before-and-after results.

4
Emerging technology

"There's no use trying," she said:
"One can't believe impossible things."

"I dare say you haven't had much practice,"
said the Queen. "When I was your age,
I always did it for half-an-hour a day.
Why, sometimes I've believed as many as
six impossible things before breakfast."

Through the Looking Glass by
Lewis Carroll (Charles Dodgson)

At a recent conference on emerging technology, a spokesman talked at length about the future of image processing, hinting that the integration of text and images would someday predict the tidal ebbs and flows of the business environment accurately. At this point, a gypsy in the audience stood up and asked "So what else is new?" Then, whipping out a crystal ball, added "we've been doing that for centuries!" Predicting the future with image technology is no more reliable than with a crystal ball, but predicting the future of image technology itself is straightforward. It requires only an understanding of what has occurred in conventional processing, in light of the factors that impact on image processing.

The significance to managers is that any system installed today should be capable of absorbing some of this emerging technology when it becomes available. The vendors themselves are moving in this direction. A seminar sponsored by IDC/Avanti Technology, held in Phoenix in January 1991, was headlined *Beyond the Obvious*, and some trade journal writers are already musing on the need for creativity as the fervor of current image technology becomes humdrum.

4.1 The technology picture

As striking as image processing technology is, arguably it has just entered the power curve section of its growth. Its present status is the result of 30 years work. The next five to ten years should witness even more significant changes, again paralleling the introduction of the integrated circuit. Many of these changes will also have been the result of extensive laboratory research that is

43

just now reaching for the commercial marketplace. For example, today's workstation that costs less than $10 thousand, would have run at least $750 thousand in 1960 (in terms of 1960 dollars). By the end of this decade, it could shrink to less than $5 thousand (at today's prices) and occupy less than 50 percent of the space. In ten years, you might be able to hold a workstation in your hand. By then, virtually every organization will be able to afford an image system.

As described in the next section, many other factors contribute to the accelerating pace of emerging technology (not counting the fascination with technology itself) that permeates much of industry and the government. Also, the government is one of the biggest users of image processing; hence by osmosis, they encourage vendors to dig deeper. But all of this is hardly unusual

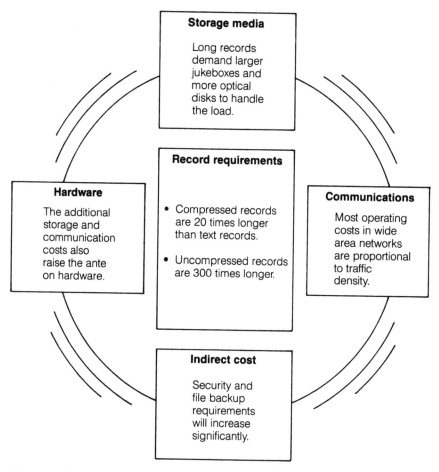

Fig. 4-1. The drive to reduce the length of records is motivated because 10 to 20 times more records exist than are now captured with data processing. Each record requires 20 times more storage space. That's a 400-to-1 ratio.

and actually is minor compared to the technological, scientific, and industrial revolution of 1895-1905.

During that period, the automobile was invented, the first large-scale mechanical computers were used, the airplane was invented, sea power came of age, psychology and psychiatry became sciences, physics was catapulted into the quantum era, and the forward pass in football was legalized (which perhaps set sports on the way to becoming a multi-billion dollar industry). By comparison, image processing seems to be tame stuff.

Oddly, much of this new technology focuses on two related goals: to reduce the length of the image record and to increase the capacity of current systems. These simple goals stem from two mathematical facts. First, roughly 20 times the amount of information now captured electronically or on microfilm begs to be acquired by image processing. Second, each record will consume an average of twenty times the storage required per page of text character records. That means a theoretical maximum increase in storage of 400. This would be like reducing the size of the Library of Congress to a small house—with room to spare.

Figure 4-1 illustrates the pattern here. The more compressed the record length becomes, the less expensive the encompassing system will be. The chief source of this compression, for text files at least, is optical character recognition—especially of handwriting. As explained in technical note C.2, this is a difficult row to hoe, but the payoff is tremendous. For the interim, portable workstations can prevent the need for some of this OCR by capturing data directly in electronic form. And none of this is too futuristic; today's state-of-the-art microcomputers easily outperform the mainframes of just 20 years ago.

4.2 Factors and trend lines

Behind this thrust to reduce record size and to improve image technology exist at least 18 factors—as structured in FIG. 4-2. The first six arise from technology itself:

- **Miniaturization.** Paralleling its counterpart in conventional processing, almost every aspect of image processing, with the obvious exception of the size of the monitor screens, is experiencing a reduction in size. In turn, this can result in lower computer or driver horsepower to enable the system to work. Further savings in space, however, at least compared to the initial savings with image system installations, are likely to be negligible.

- **Cost reduction.** The price of just about every element associated with image processing is declining. This element has been part of the history of data processing since its inception, and there is no reason to believe it will stop.

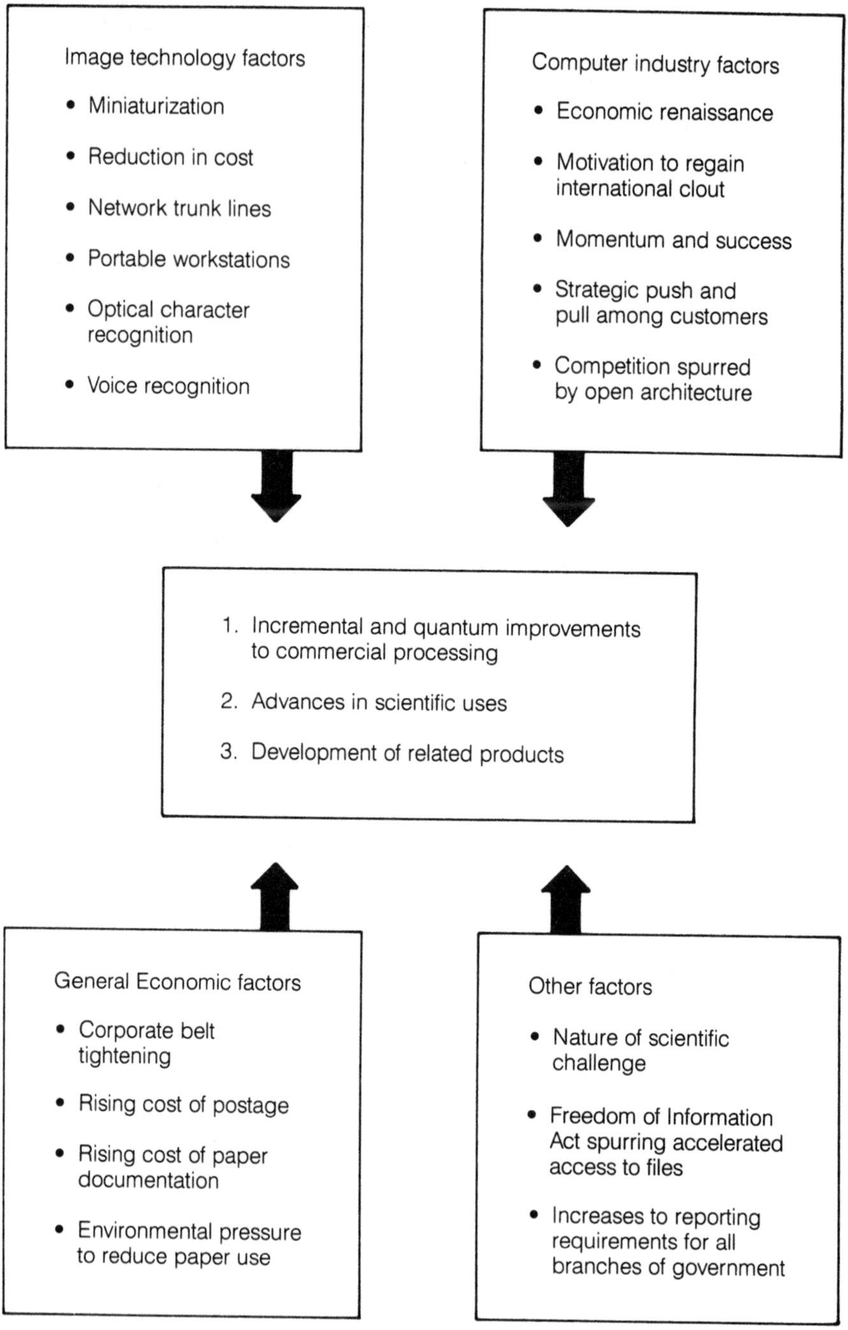

Image technology factors

- Miniaturization

- Reduction in cost

- Network trunk lines

- Portable workstations

- Optical character recognition

- Voice recognition

Computer industry factors

- Economic renaissance

- Motivation to regain international clout

- Momentum and success

- Strategic push and pull among customers

- Competition spurred by open architecture

1. Incremental and quantum improvements to commercial processing

2. Advances in scientific uses

3. Development of related products

General Economic factors

- Corporate belt tightening

- Rising cost of postage

- Rising cost of paper documentation

- Environmental pressure to reduce paper use

Other factors

- Nature of scientific challenge

- Freedom of Information Act spurring accelerated access to files

- Increases to reporting requirements for all branches of government

Fig. 4-2. At least 18 factors have combined to accelerate the development of image processing technology—and most of these factors are beyond the reasons of sustaining what already exists.

- **Wide-area network extreme high-density trunk lines.** Eventually, high-density communications trunk lines will be able to carry traffic between computers and other stations—as if they were integral units of a single computer. This is especially important for image processing because of the long record lengths and the resulting pressure to distribute storage in systems where central storage could be more efficient and contribute to improved interior lines.

- **Portable workstations.** Workstations (a FAX machine/scanner, laser printer, computer, flat screen, and a cellular phone) will be compressed into the size of an attaché case. Actually, units similar to this are already used by the military and are built to withstand rugged handling. Paperwork will be eliminated in proportion to the availability of these workstations.

- **Advances in optical character recognition (OCR).** OCR technology is largely confined to characters intentionally designed for this purpose and to some typewriter/printer fonts. But as previewed above, the motivation to decipher the handwriting on the form is exceptionally strong. The U.S. Postal Service is also working on this technology.

- **Advances in voice recognition.** *Voice recognition*, the conversion of voice input into digital data, is a proven technology, but its potential for use with image processing is just now being implemented. The potential, however, is unlimited, ranging from executives making memo notations to the approval process for claims and other transactions.

The next five factors have arisen from within the computer industry. Some of these factors have always been present, and others are strongly related to the advent of practical image processing:

- **A renaissance for the computer industry.** The sagging fortunes of much of the computer industry are being boosted by image technology. For example, IBM did not hesitate to invest billions in it, once it recognized the potential. The Forbes magazine cover story article, cited in section 1.7, is further evidence of this.

- **Momentum and success.** Image processing has caught on so well and so fast that some vendors have a difficult time keeping up with the traffic. This situation could encourage sloppy work, but so far the opposite seems to be true even though the work is increasing at an exponential rate.

- **The pressure to regain international economic leverage.** It is no secret that the United States has lost some of its competitive edge in world markets, especially in electronics. Even image processing gained popularity earlier in other countries before it did in the U.S. Image processing offers a major opportunity to regain it, despite that Pacific basin countries took the lead more than a decade ago.

- **Strategic push and pull.** The corporations and agencies that are first with image processing are pushing technology, and the balance of the competition will be pulled into the maelstrom just to keep pace. Perhaps it has always been this way, but the image processing momentum accelerates the process.

- **Open architectural environment.** Most vendors have maintained an open architectural marketing approach, insofar as the realities of hardware and software permit. This stance has encouraged new partnerships among them. In turn, this seems to accelerate technological research even more strongly than the strategic push and pull factor.

The next four factors are economic in nature, although this in no way suggests that the other factors are without economic ramifications.

- **Corporate belt tightening.** In anticipation of a major recession, corporate America has been cutting costs recently. Approximately 300,000 middle managers were let go in 1990. These companies would not hesitate to cut costs further as the economic advantages of image processing are recognized.

- **The rising cost of postage.** First class mail is now 29 cents per letter, and somewhat less for bulk mailing. Estimates for the year 2000 are in the range of 50 cents per letter. Note that perhaps 80 percent of first class mail is business related, and most of that is composed of bills and payments.

- **The cost of paper.** The cost of paper is increasing, and as the number of documents increase, so will the total bill for it. This factor applies both to the paper itself and the increasing need for it.

- **Environmental pressures.** In addition to the cost of paper, environmental pressures to conserve forests, combined with only limited ability to recycle used paper, will further discourage the use of paper. Also, 50% of landfill waste is paper.

The last three factors are miscellaneous in nature, but still deserve attention.

- **The nature of scientific challenge.** Leaders in technological research are motivated by exceptional challenges, especially when they have commercial backing for products with scientific uses.

- **Freedom of Information Act.** This piece of legislation is motivating many government agencies to streamline their documentation filing and retrieval procedures.

- **Legal challenges.** All three branches of government are increasing their surveillance of business operations—from those in aircraft maintenance to bank load portfolios. This usually translates into increased reporting. Image processing systems are an obvious means of reducing the burden.

4.3 Significance for commercial applications

The factors discussed in the previous section lead without much trouble to a number of conclusions in terms of practical applications.

- **Greater affordability.** A system that cost one million dollars today could be available for $200 thousand (at today's prices) within five years, and similarly, one that cost $200 thousand today could go for $40 thousand within five years.

- **Distal workstations.** Portable workstations will likely lead to acquiring image information on-the-spot. For example, a number of municipal courts employ image processing systems to store traffic citations (case B.8), but those citations begin with the familiar ticket. To eliminate even that paper, and speed up the filing process further, it is conceivable that portable specialized recording and acquisition technology will be built into portable cellular phones, complete with a small thermal printer to give the offenders a "receipt."

- **User image document repositories.** Although early predictions of checkless banking failed, the crushing load of checks and the cost of billing and payment by mail could encourage corporations and utilities to set up monthly fixed-fee billing direct to checking accounts, with updates to vector image records that customers could dial up and print on home computer systems. Fixed periodic billing is in use in many locations; this merely expands the practice to image processing. What's more, this concept could be extended to preparing income tax returns. When verified or corrected by the individual, the returns could be forwarded electronically to the IRS. Conceivably, the government could even offer economic incentives to encourage the process, which would be paid for with the savings that it would generate for itself (see FIG. 4-3).

- **Image libraries.** Books and other publications are growing, and growing more expensive by the day—perhaps fueled by the proliferation of word processing software and the publish-or-perish syndrome that permeates university faculties. It is only a matter of time before most of

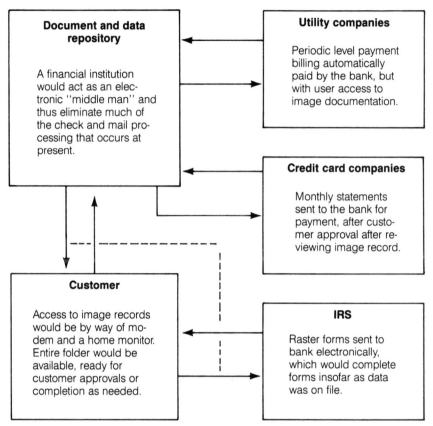

Fig. 4-3. Although the promise of checkless banking did not materialize with data processing, image processing could give the concept new life by way of storing customer images and digital data in one system—motivated by economic incentives.

this material, including most of the indexes, is fully automated in terms of image storage. In that way, any number of users could access the same material at the same time. Early versions will have read-only optical disks distributed to libraries. In time, material will be accessed from central locations, improving the currency of the data.

- **Instant tailor-made publishing.** You have heard about desktop publishing. Now meet son-of-desktop-publishing—the instant, tailor-made book. This practice is already formalized at a number of institutions, where professors and instructors draw from selected materials and generate specialized books for specific classes and purposes (usually by arrangement with the various copyright holders). Still, this process generates paper, so the logical extension would be to produce optical chips that would be inserted in electronic clipboards, described in section 4.5.

4.4 Significance for scientific applications

The potential for scientific applications is even greater than for commercial applications, although the number of installations will probably be far fewer in number. Moreover, many of these applications will be based on vector images, that is, the generation of images from data (FIG. 4-4). Many, if not most, will be dynamic—in effect motion pictures. A few are described here:

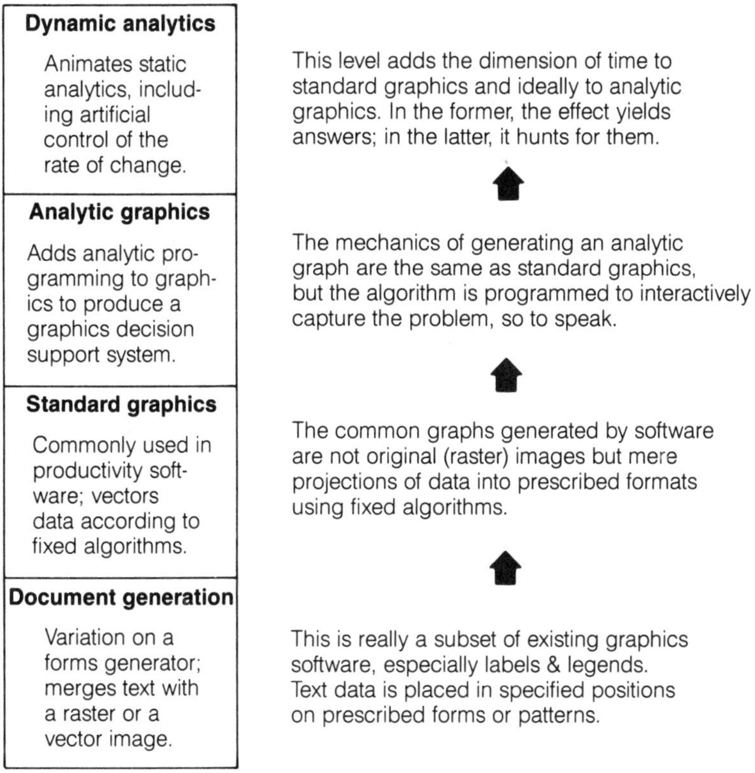

Dynamic analytics

Animates static analytics, including artificial control of the rate of change.

This level adds the dimension of time to standard graphics and ideally to analytic graphics. In the former, the effect yields answers; in the latter, it hunts for them.

Analytic graphics

Adds analytic programming to graphics to produce a graphics decision support system.

The mechanics of generating an analytic graph are the same as standard graphics, but the algorithm is programmed to interactively capture the problem, so to speak.

Standard graphics

Commonly used in productivity software; vectors data according to fixed algorithms.

The common graphs generated by software are not original (raster) images but mere projections of data into prescribed formats using fixed algorithms.

Document generation

Variation on a forms generator; merges text with a raster or a vector image.

This is really a subset of existing graphics software, especially labels & legends. Text data is placed in specified positions on prescribed forms or patterns.

Fig. 4-4. The hierarchy of vector imaging. For all their simplicity, even vector images use four levels, the first two of which are used in or with commercial image systems. The other two, for the most part, are used for scientific applications.

- **Medical science.** Three-dimensional imagery for diagnosis and for simulated medical research is already a reality, and the potential for mapping the entire human physiology and genetics is just a matter of time. Within 10 or 15 years, the entire gene code could be deciphered and eventually built into these models. The significance is that what now takes years and even decades to analyze might soon be done in hours and days. Offshoots of this technology will probably include baseline images developed for individuals, which could then be used to detect the early presence of many diseases and other maladies.

- **Engineering and ecology.** Image processing, in many forms, is already used in engineering design work, but not greatly to analyze long-term maintenance problems or the effects of major designs and layouts on the environment. Like the applications for medical science, the potential here is enormous. However, many generations must pass before any model can be certified as being truly representative of the environment. The demand for this type of system could have a higher priority than medical systems, as a result of the larger number of people affected by most questions.

- **Physics.** One of the most pressing problems in physics is the inability of equations to precisely measure the effects of three or more bodies acting on one another. As a result, mathematical physics is really an approximation of what occurs in nature (e.g. movements of the planets). These "approximations" are good enough for most purposes, but when it comes to analysis in subatomic physics, where the number of bodies/ particles is in the millions, the mathematical challenge becomes insurmountable. Image processing can solve this problem by controlling the movement of each item and generating a dynamic image of an entire system. Again, each hypothesized example must be verified, but in time the models will become accurate.

- **Education.** The potential for instantly customized dynamic learning materials tailored to each student's needs is unlimited. The great problem of single teachers trying to individualize instruction for classes of 30 to 35 students, sometimes higher, could be overcome. True, early attempts at programmed instruction were largely failures, and audio/ visuals were often little more than enhanced lectures. This system is different, however. The ability to access vast stores of information or to seek help for common learning problems would be virtually unlimited.

4.5 Significance for related vendor products

The image processing field, like laser technology 30 years ago, overflows with the potential for new products that are either unrelated or only distantly related to permanent document storage. Some of these are gadgets, many of which will flounder in the marketplace. Still, the potential exists and given the spectrum of junk available in stores today, the ideas are not all bad.

- **Electronic clipboards.** Instead of photocopying umpteen copies of memos for distribution and comment, which uses up tons of paper and keeps photocopy machine repairmen in the chips, copies could be circulated on erasable programmable (rewritable or EPROM) chips and inserted in "clipboards" with solid-state screens. Alternatively, the data could be distributed via a local network and recorded in the "clipboard."

- **Automated travel atlases and tourguides.** Auto clubs commonly provide customized route planning, complete with maps and often with books on accommodations and attractions. At the same time, palmtop computers can display some data to aid travelers. Image processing offers the opportunity to put the entire system on a chip that can be inserted in an electronic clipboard described above. Then, with optimizing software, various routes (scenic, most direct, etc.) would pop up instantly on the screen. An alternative version of this would draw the most current information by modem (see FIG. 4-5).

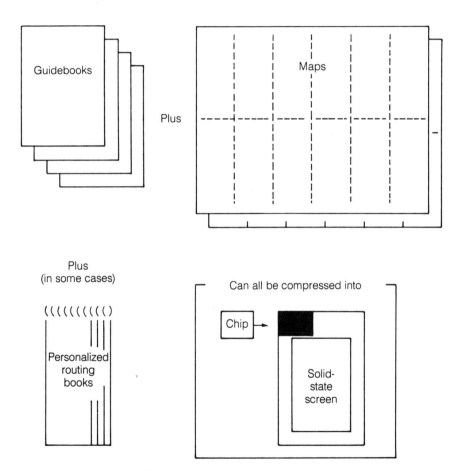

Fig. 4-5. Most automobile clubs inundate their members with travel books and maps. Image processing technology could reduce all of it to a clipboard and a chip. Alternatively, the data could be distributed by telephone and modem.

- **Automated catalogues.** These catalogues are a variation on the automated travel atlas, and the automated image library described in section 4.3. The cost of printing and distributing these catalogues is enormous. Hence, recording these on chips for display in a computer or "clipboard" could eventually be less expensive than using paper. Customers could also get instant displays of any type of item and develop an order message in the process.

- **Three dimensional television.** The technology to generate three-dimensional images by holography has been in existence for more than 10 years. A notable example is displayed in the computer center at Epcot Center in Disney World, Orlando, Florida. A variation of this was displayed at the 1990 COMDEX trade show in Las Vegas, Nevada. A computer-generated three-dimensional image was projected around the viewer who wore a special helmet.

- **Consumer finance.** This potential application could be accomplished entirely with data processing, but the addition of dynamic vector images could sell it better. The ability to project the effects of many financial decisions into dynamic graphs would help many consumers with their choices and investments.

- **Home computers.** The renewed attempt to market conventional computers for home use by at least three major vendors could again sputter. There is very little need for data processing in a home environment—no matter how user friendly the software gets or how low the price reduces to. Image processing is a different story. Most households are plagued with paperwork that ranges from income tax returns to recipe files. Low-price desktop image systems could open a whole new market.

4.6 Side effects

Few technologies have grown without side effects, some are beneficial, but others are indisputably negative. Image technology is not an exception. Understandably, no vendor wants to harp on the subject, and many of the side effects are beyond any individual's or any corporation's control. Still, they will not likely evaporate:

- **Widespread unemployment.** The major cost savings from image technology must come from somewhere, and that somewhere is by laying off of hundreds of thousands, perhaps millions, of employees. Some of these jobs will be absorbed by the requirement for more skilled workers to run the system; however, as the number of installations expand, the layoffs will accumulate. More than 300 thousand white collar work-

ers were laid off during 1990, so few companies will pass up the opportunity to lay off even more employees, especially if the current recession
deepens. In turn, the welfare and unemployment compensation costs
will rise and so will taxes to pay for them. Thus, the costs saved could
be negated by these higher taxes. Labor unions could reverse their long
decline in popularity by using the "job-preservation ticket." Incidentally, this union policy would also cover many middle managers who
presently oversee manual record-keeping functions.

• **The massing of enormous amounts of automated information.** Abuse of information accesses generated by data processing systems has led to an increasing number of restrictions. The potential to
automate 20 times the amount of information now available on systems
or microforms can only intensify the abuses and bring far more stringent regulation. A simple example of this, although it did not involve
commercial image processing, was the announcement by Lotus Development Corporation to sell consumer information CD-ROM discs (as
reported in the *Wall Street Journal*, November 13, 1990, B1,B9). The
complete set of discs would have listed the names, addresses, shopping
tendencies, and probable income levels of approximately 80 million U.S.
households. Critics concede that the information is already available
collectively from numerous sources, but the cost of getting and compil-
ing it would be prohibitive. The Lotus product would have changed this.
For roughly $6.4 million, any corporation could have bought the works
(or pay $400 per five thousand names) without any controls on how it
uses the data. The price might seem high to an individual, but it was
petty cash in terms of major advertising accounts. Fortunately, the negative publicity persuaded Lotus to abandon the project.

• **Exponential increases in required reports for the government.** The ability to access multitudes of documents will undoubtedly
encourage the federal government to demand more reports on every
conceivable subject of interest, and virtually everything that goes on in
a corporation is of interest to some government agency somewhere.
Moreover, since these reports would be submitted on disk, these agencies would claim that paperwork is being reduced—even though the
number of reports would actually be increasing.

• **Decline of the commercial real estate market.** In most cities,
the commercial real estate market is already depressed. Freeing massive storage areas could make matters worse. It is not at all unusual for a
single image system installation to free from 50 thousand to 100 thousand square feet of space.

• **Commercial couch potatoes.** As much drudgery as was involved
with digging up information to solve business problems, the effort at least

forced executives to leave their offices occasionally. But when every possible piece of information is instantly available on a terminal, the temptation to operate primarily from a desk could become irresistible.

The potential side effects are not all negative, of course. At least one, the accelerated redistribution of the workforce, appears to offer major advantages. If the workforce is redistributed away from the cities, the massive social problems of having large compressed populations could be deintensified. This is no small consideration, and eventually it could also reduce the cost of living.

4.7 Some philosophical considerations

The theoretical end point of emerging technology is the human brain. Everything that a system costing $10 million can do can be done by those few pounds of protoplasm that are worth about $10 of plentiful elements. It might not be as fast, but it can store millions of images, retrieve and relate most of them instantly, and even zoom in on particulars—all in an unbeatably user-friendly environment. We don't give it a second thought. So, the future applications mentioned in this chapter will hardly make a dent in this potential. What's more, the unfortunate condition of autistic savants (who display awesome computer powers) and the unusual capabilities of numerous animals suggest that the potential is even greater than we see in a so-called normal organism.

For example, the Navy has yet to duplicate the efficiency of the sonar possessed by dolphins, and no one has been able to duplicate the fantastic radar of bats—at least not in that small a space. Then there is the unusual but documented, capability of shelties (Shetland Sheepdogs) to sometimes detect the approach of their masters from more than a mile away. Assuming that this phenomenon has a down-to-earth explanation, it is reasonable to assume that each individual radiates a certain pattern of reflected magnetic fields. There's no question about that, really. Neutron magnetic resonance has relied on it for years. But if the signals are still distinguishable at a distance of a mile by biological receptors, what kind of medically significant information can be detected from a few inches away?

For this reason, the introduction to this book suggests that the scientific applications for image systems will someday take precedence over the commercial variety, at least in terms of research and development. The challenge is tougher, and within 20 years, if not sooner, just about every organization that can benefit from these commercial systems will have the technology.

Part II

Set-up

Fifty years separate the Kodak Ektra 35mm camera and the optical disk system 6800 automated library (or jukebox as it is commonly called). Arguably, each represents the epitome of its time, but like most landmark technology, serves primarily as a model for better things to come. Fewer than 2,500 of the Ektras were sold, yet every one of its features is now standard on one or more high-grade cameras at 10 percent of the cost (adjusted for inflation). Similarly, the features of the 6800 will undoubtedly have higher capacities at faster speeds in smaller spaces. They will probably be manufactured by at least one

Fig. II-1. The Kodak Ekta camera. (Courtesy Eastman Kodak)

half-dozen vendors. But none of this progress is or will be worth much if the database structure and the processing imposed on it are inadequate. That is, the hardware technology provides opportunities, not solutions. Those solutions are the product of disciplined analysis.

The components of image technology work extremely well, but the image system's effectiveness depends on the configuration and set-up of those components—from jukebox to software.

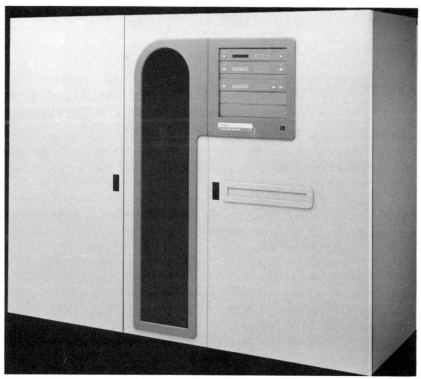

Fig. II-2. The model 6800 Optical Disk Library. (Courtesy Eastman Kodak)

5

Structure and storage

*The modern age has a false sense of superiority
because it relies on the mass of knowledge that
it can use, but what is important is the extent
to which knowledge is organized and mastered.*

Goethe, 1810

Image records are larger than their digital counterparts by one, two, and even three orders of magnitude. Worse, most corporations and institutions must manage 10 times more paper documents than the digital form. What's more, the necessity to link different records from different electronic folders often imposes tougher indexing requirements than occurs with data processing. Then, effective image processing systems begin with effective structures. This truth is easier said than done.

First, the write-once-read-many (WORM) feature of most optical disk drivers prevents rearranging records, except by expensive recompilation on new disks (although the separate index files on magnetic storage can be modified). Second, verifying correct recordings is more complex. Third, attribute data (data used to manage the records) is often updated after the records are acquired, but not always on the records themselves. True, no one of these requirements is overwhelming, but the sheer mass imposes complex tasks.

This chapter addresses those tasks with a review of the types of images, a macro view of magnitudes, an outline of some indexing and linkage options, and a description of alternative storage media (in more detail than covered in chapter 3). At the end of the chapter is a recap on the life cycle of an image record and a separate section that describes the miscellaneous factors that affect image records.

5.1 Types of images

An image is an image, correct? Not so, at least not in terms of the way they are stored. Four different spectral types are encountered in image systems: *bilevels*, *halftones*, *graytones* (spelled *greytones* by some vendors), and *color*. Each has its own storage requirements and most can benefit from different algorithms for compression. Additionally, the degree of resolution (dots or pix-

60   Structure and storage

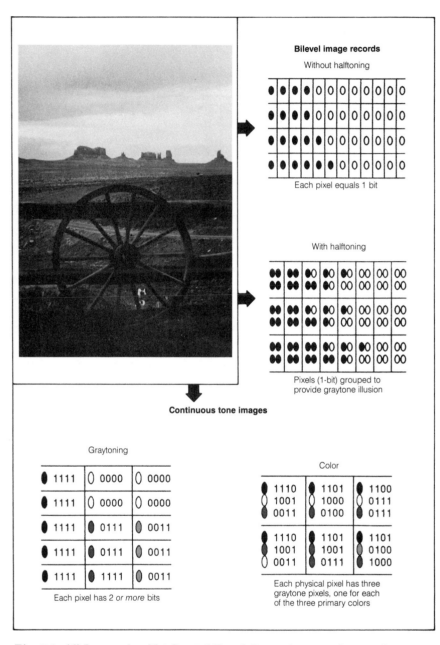

Fig. 5-1. All Images Are Not Created Equal. Image is a generic term that covers different types, which absorb increasing amounts of space. The impact on costs by using a mixture of these types is so great that senior executives understand the differences.

els per inch) will affect record length (technical note C.1). Figure 5-1 illustrates
the mechanics.

- **Bilevel image records.** A *bilevel* (or *bitonal*) is the replacement term
  for black-and-white. The reason is that any color can be used for the
  foreground, and any contrasting color for the background without
  affecting record length or structure. A dot of foreground material is
  stored as the value 1 in a bit of memory. Background material is stored
  as a 0; i.e., it is not recorded. The image can be displayed or printed in
  any foreground color that a monitor displays or ink that a printer uses.

- **Halftone image records.** *Halftoning* is a method of producing the
  illusion of shades of gray by blocking units of bilevel bits. In a 2×2
  matrix with the individual bits imperceptible to the human eye, white
  (the absence of color) is represented by four 0s; black (or any solid
  color), by four 1s; and three apparent shades of gray (or whatever color
  results from mixing the primaries), by one, two, or three 1s. Technically,
  a halftone is bilevel, but compression algorithms used to store bilevel
  text-images are not effective for storing pictorial halftones. These techniques can even increase storage requirements (see technical note C.3)
  for pictorial halftones.

- **Graytone image records.** *Graytoning*, sometimes called *continuous
  toning*, uses two or more bits per dot. Thus, each dot represents either
  of two colors or any shade between as a function of the number of bits
  used to store each dot. One byte (8 bits) yields 254 shades not counting
  the polemics, which is more than necessary to store ordinary images,
  but inadequate for some scientific work. Graytone images are memory-
  hungry, and the storage algorithms sacrifice some detail.

- **Color image records.** Color imaging is graytoning extended to three
  dots of information per physical dot on the image. If you photograph a
  color scene with black-and-white "slide" film and red, blue, and green
  filters, the three images projected on a screen (using the same filters)
  will generate a color image. Honest!

5.2 Dimensions and magnitudes

As implied in the previous section, the more pictorial an image is, and the
more refinement that is necessary, the longer the stored record will be. Longer
records mean larger optical disk library hardware and transmission costs;
however, this has little impact on workstations and only minorly affects scanners and printers (except for large engineering drawings). In analogous terms,

image processing is Gulliver visiting Lilliput, and a high concentration of pictorial matter is equal to a regiment of Gulliver's.

The common unit of measure is the *pel* (or *pixel*), the picture element that is usually expressed in units per inch. Thus, 200 pels means 200 dots per inch. The horizontal resolution is usually expressed before the vertical. Hence, 300 × 200 means 300 pels per inch horizontally and 200 lines per inch vertically. If only one number is given, the implication is that it covers both directions. In practice, 200 × 200 resolution is the norm for most documents. Higher densities are used in special cases, and the lower density of 100x100 is sometimes used for less-important records that have no legal significance.

The fortunate aspect of using the 200x200 resolution is that is does not necessarily require four times the record length of 100 × 100 resolution. True, the image as originally scanned has four times as many pels, but compression algorithms eliminate much of the excess baggage. Technical note C.3 describes these algorithms in more detail. In essence, a "line" of image (technically a raster, is the height of one unit of vertical resolution) is compressed into segments of one color or the other. Then, subsequent lines are recorded only as changes to the previous compressed record. Because text images rarely change from foreground to background color every dot, 500 thousand bytes of information can be reduced to 30 thousand bytes or so. But pictorial images, because the dot pattern changes far more frequently, seldom benefit from this logical packaging. Sometimes, the compression requires more storage.

This algorithm became standard as the FAX machine gained popularity (the total reaching towards three million today). Since transmission was expensive, economic necessity dictated that the record be compressed. Because the receiver had to decompress the compressed image, economic necessity also led to standardization. This algorithm (actually, there are several minor variations) also works for imaging. A scanner is, in effect, a FAX machine and the optical disk is merely a means of storing the image between the equivalents of sending (acquisition) and receiving (access).

In practice, some scanners divide images into blocks, called *tiling*, and others use sophisticated software to screen out "noise." Noise is any speck or other disruption on a document (including a tear) that should not be there, but still consumes memory. Other scanners can differentiate between text and pictures and apply different levels of resolution, create compound documents, or alternatively, separate the document into separate blocks for different levels of resolution. All of these features cost more, but if they can reduce storage requirements significantly, they will quickly pay for themselves.

Now the senior executive rightfully asks, "Just how much detail must I master before I reach the point of diminishing return on the power curve of technical knowledge?" The answer is: enough to ensure that technical staffers know what they are doing and that vendors sell you what you need, neither excessively sophisticated nor underpowered for your needs. Technological options are expanding at lightning speed and with a dazzle that tends to wash out essential details. To continue with the detail, then, TABLE 5-1 provides comparative data on image storage requirements, from which it is easy to see why large systems require very high capacity jukeboxes.

Table 5-1. Image Magnitudes. Pictorial images need longer records because of less-efficient compression algorithms. Graytoning can raise the ante by a factor of 4 (or more), and color by a factor of 24 (or more). The larger the total storage requirement, the higher the cost. In practice, the increases do not always rise in direct proportion, but the comparative totals are still convincing enough to avoid treating every record as graytone. Assume a compression ratio of 15:1 and a document size of 8.5 inches by 11 inches. For continuous tone, assume one byte per pixel. For color images, multiply the graytone totals by three.

| Number of records | Bilevel | | Graytone |
	Without compression	With compression	
100	46,750,000	3,116,667	374,000,000
1,000	467,500,000	31,166,667	3,740,000,000
10,000	4,675,000,000	311,666,667	37,400,000,000
50,000	23,375,000,000	1,558,333,333	187,000,000,000
100,000	46,750,000,000	3,116,666,667	374,000,000,000
500,000	233,750,000,000	15,583,333,333	1,870,000,000,000
1,000,000	467,500,000,000	31,166,666,667	3,740,000,000,000
10,000,000	4,675,000,000,000	311,666,666,667	37,400,000,000,000
50,000,000	23,375,000,000,000	1,558,333,333,333	187,000,000,000,000
100,000,000	46,750,000,000,000	3,116,666,666,667	374,000,000,000,000

5.3 Indexing, folders and linkage

As a bare minimum, every document that is stored in an image system must be indexed. The alternative of naming them and running a sequential search for each access is untenable for all but toy installations. Beyond this minimum, most installations require additional information to support processing, retention, priorities, and other requirements. These add-ons are called *attributes*. Attributes can be stored as part of the record on an optical disk, a separate disk, or on separate magnetic storage. The simplest arrangement includes them with the record and then duplicates the indexing information on fast-access magnetic storage. Unfortunately, this system prevents subsequent updates on WORM-type optical disks. A more usable alternative puts a permanent label on the record, which then links all attribute information on magnetic disk.

In practice, most systems come packaged with software and procedures for entering attribute information, so most of the options are usually moot. What is important is that users are able to assemble related documents by entering a minimum number of instructions on the keyboard. The most common of these methods is to create an electronic folder that automatically links and retrieves related documents. Here, the user retrieves the folder, rather than specific documents. Once retrieved, only the relevant pages in the folder need to be scanned. Other systems link folders to electronic drawers and then to electronic cabinets. On the other hand, many customers have discovered that existing manual indexing and coding algorithms work best.

The key, then, is to identify what handles are necessary. In theory, this should follow from a detailed analysis of requirements. As many analysts are unaware of the complexity of records management, a good understanding of the potential items often helps. However, all of them should not necessarily be included in each case; of those that are required, some can be read by bar code or pattern recognition. Other data can be entered by default, to be revised only on an exception basis. Still other data can be computer generated. Without respect to the method of capture, these items include but are no means limited to:

- Type of file and/or document
- Folder and other direct linkage information
- Description and notes
- Date and time of acquisition
- Dates and times of subsequent updates (and action taken)
- Processing priority codes
- Type of file and/or document
- Retention and/or destruction date codes
- Routing and processing required codes
- Codes for downgrading storage status

This list might seem intimidating, but it merely reflects what is done manually, often by record clerks who work with memorized procedures. An image system must automate this logic in part and create clear dividing lines between automated processing and manual intervention (FIG. 5-2).

5.4 Storage media

Section 3.2 describes the three common levels of image-record storage: magnetic disk, on-line optical disk, and off-line optical disk. To some extent, this was misleading. Image records can be stored on any media, including punch

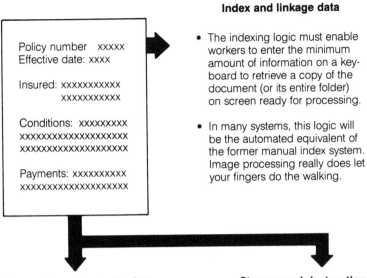

Index and linkage data

Policy number   xxxxx
Effective date: xxxx

Insured: xxxxxxxxxxx
        xxxxxxxxxxx

Conditions: xxxxxxxxx
xxxxxxxxxxxxxxxxxxxx
xxxxxxxxxxxxxxxxxxxx

Payments: xxxxxxxxxx
xxxxxxxxxxxxxxxxxxxx

- The indexing logic must enable workers to enter the minimum amount of information on a keyboard to retrieve a copy of the document (or its entire folder) on screen ready for processing.

- In many systems, this logic will be the automated equivalent of the former manual index system. Image processing really does let your fingers do the walking.

Processing and priority data

- All processing and priority attribute data is optional, analogous to a life jacket upon abandoning ship.

- The idea is to level out the queues, keep the workloads distributed, and above all get things done on time.

Storage and destruction data

- Every document must be stored somewhere and in most cases will change venue one or more times in its image lifetime.

- Most (but not all) records eventually will be destroyed on a schedule, else the system would become overloaded.

Fig. 5-2. Image systems have automated a horde of manual procedures and attribute data. Of the three generic categories depicted here, processing and priority data are the most complex.

cards, magnetic tape, microfilm, and sea shells.* However, the only practical alternative (just now coming on the market) is optical tape, which is similar to magnetic tape. Optical tape is especially useful for storing image records that are seldom accessed or for a security backup for optical disks.

Because on-line and off-line optical disks differ only in the mechanics of getting the disk into a driver, and because magnetic disk storage is well understood, attention is usually focused on the optical disk itself. They are round,

---

* The sea shell option has been used once, to prove a point at the headquarters of Wang Laboratories in Lowell, Massachusetts. A photograph of the late An Wang was scanned and the graytone data recorded in an enlarged matrix. Miniature sea shells of different shades were then glued on the matrix to correspond to the data for each pel.

but beyond that nothing is standard. Three common diameters (5.25 inch, 12 inch, and 14 inch) are available. At least four different surfaces and laser etching processes are used (technical note C.4). Disks can be read only (CD-ROM), write-once-read-many (WORM), or erasable (which has many names). Then, too, different drivers format disks in different ways, and not all systems use the same compression algorithms, especially for graytone and color images.

The optical disk library unit (the jukebox). Some are single drive models in which the user inserts a disk. Others house hundreds of disks and can store more than a trillion bytes (a terabyte) of information. Size, weight, cost, warranty, and data transfer speed vary considerably for jukeboxes; the first four of these factors also vary considerably for disks. Fortunately, this awesome range of choices is seldom a problem. The size of the proposed system, in combination with the products offered by the vendors, narrow the choices. The one point that managers must understand are the differences among the three types of disks:

- **Read-only memory (ROM or CD-ROM).** This is a variation on the common CD. Information is embedded on the disk at the time of manufacture and cannot be readily changed afterwards. It is useless for saving documents. However, it is an inexpensive means for recording software or other permanent information, such as forms over which text data can be superimposed to form a vector image.

- **Write-once read-many (WORM).** *WORM* is the workhorse of image systems. As the name implies, once the image record is recorded, it is more or less permanent. Unfortunately, the bits that are not marked can be marked later and modify or totally obliterate some records.

- **Rewritable.** This third type is quickly gaining popularity. It offers the flexibility of updating attribute data and also being reused when existing records are discarded. The negative is that the stored records would have a tougher time gaining acceptance in court as evidence, a point covered in chapter 11. Also, it is easier to accidentally erase these records.

All of these characteristics are subject to technological advances, most notably the increase in storage capacity per track and the number of tracks per disk of the same size. In early 1991, for example, Eastman Kodak announced that its 14-inch disk, which stored 6.8 billion bytes (gigabytes), will now store 10.2 billion. This means that any particular system could increase its capacity by 50 percent for very little cost. In combination with the promise of new compression algorithms, especially for picture-type images, this is important. (TABLE 5-2)

Most optical disks are warranted to store records reliably for a minimum of 10 years (and some up to 30 years) under prescribed conditions of humidity and temperature. Perhaps they are good for 50 years or even longer; only experience will tell. Another interesting problem is the effect of technology on records that must be stored for 20 years or more. Twenty years from now, the current operating machines might no longer be available to read those disks. If this is correct, then the need to transfer records to other media, perhaps to optical tape or microform, will become more important than extending the shelf life of recorded disks.

Table 5-2. Optical disk capacities are awesome, but then so are record lengths and the number of records that must be stored. This data records storage space on the three common sizes of disks. All computations are based on the data and assumptions listed in Table 5-1.

Type of record	5.25-Inch Disk 900 Megabytes	12-Inch Disk 6,500 Megabytes	14-Inch Disk 10,200 Megabytes
BiLevel Compressed	28,877	208,556	327,273
BiLevel Uncompressed	1,925	13,903	27,817
Graytone	240	1,737	2,720
Color	80	579	907

5.5 The life cycle of image records

The preceding discussions can be recapped by looking at the typical life cycle of an image record, from paper document to destruction (FIG. 5-3). In most cases, the original paper document is destroyed after an interim period set aside to support resolution of any acquisition errors. In some cases, the document must be stored for a longer period because of legal requirements. From that point forward, the "original" document is a "dehydrated" electronic bitstream that makes no sense to the computer. This bitstream can be "reconstituted" to form an image that can be interpreted by human perception and reprinted if necessary.

5.6 Additional factors

A wide range of factors affect the efficiency and productivity of an image system, and many of these defy neat categorization. Some are an inherent side-effect of the technology; others tend to be serious only during installation. In the latter case, early resolution is imperative, and therefore problems don't remain for long. Both anchor to the structure of the image database and record attributes.

The simplest of these factors arise from the decision to combine acquisition and initial processing at each workstation, or to separate these two steps into different divisions. Hordes of arguments support either approach, and both are in common use—even in the same type of application. The decision, however, will normally impact the way the attributes are organized. Separate acquisition stations can, under some circumstances, require more sophisticated attributes.

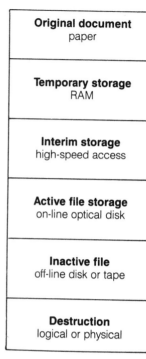

Original document paper	Image systems get rid of paper mediums but keep the information and data.
Temporary storage RAM	This stage is used primarily to check the reliability of the image record.
Interim storage high-speed access	The intense document processing occurs during the first few days after entry.
Active file storage on-line optical disk	This stage is what most organizations refer to as records management.
Inactive file off-line disk or tape	As in manual systems, inactive records are moved to less expensive space.
Destruction logical or physical	WORM disks should be destroyed; rewritable disks erased or rewritten.

Fig. 5-3. The Life Cycle of an Image Record. Most image system records progress through six stages after the paper document arrives. Some systems bypass one or more of the stages, and some divide the initial processing stage into several sub-stages.

The next factor concerns the management of the system—the software and coding used: to account for productivity, to redistribute workloads according to employee skill levels or to accommodate peak or unusual loads, to keep tabs on who accesses particular records, to increase priority codes when documents remain in queue too long, and to verify the accuracy of the recorded image (always necessary to some degree). In many ways, this entails optimization routines, or what is formally called *linear programming*. When it doesn't, the reports need to be simple enough for supervisors to take immediate action and not be forced to thumb through a procedural volume. Closely associated are the problems of controlling concurrent processing and document generation. Image processing permits concurrent access to any document, but in practice much of the processing is dependent on previous input.

It doesn't end here. Part III of this book covers a number of issues that hover over most image systems. The resolution of all of them will have some impact on the structure and attributes of an image database. The point is that the structural design of the database drives an image system from a logical viewpoint; all of the factors that can and will affect the database should be addressed before that structure is solidified. It will pay handsome dividends.

6

Acquisition, access and networks

You push the button, and we do the rest.

Former slogan of Eastman Kodak

The man-machine interface, what scientists call *ergonomics*, arguably has been the most challenging problem in computer-based systems, and image processing takes no holiday here. Photography offers a good analogy. Most cameras are simple to operate and can perform wonders under adverse conditions. The user simply aims the camera and presses a button. However, the content and usefulness of the resulting photos are another matter, not to mention how they are organized and stored once developed.

The same problem occurs in image processing systems. One can slip document after document under the scanner, but if they are entered at a slight skew and the scanner does not correct for it (or reject the document), the compression algorithm would no longer work efficiently. This error would significantly increase storage requirements, perhaps by as much as twofold. From that point forward, a dozen more pitfalls await the unwary, not the least of which is failing to scan the back side of a document or skipping a page. In short, careful attention to acquisition procedures and hardware can make the most of a good image database structure. In turn, this attention will nearly eliminate access problems and make it easier for efficient network configurations.

6.1 Acquisition

Scanners are available in many shapes, sizes, speeds, reliabilities, prices, and so forth (FIG. 6-1). Strangely enough, the temptation to overbuy capability here is sometimes justified because acquisition is the most error-prone phase of imaging. Better technology can reduce the error rate, but not eliminate it. However, do not change from one mode of scanning to another. Each type has its advantages and disadvantages. They are not interchangeable, in the practical sense, for any given system.

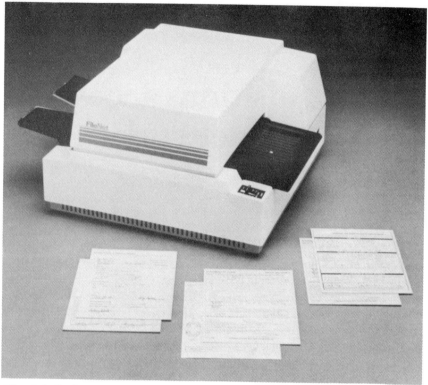

Fig. 6-1. Desktop scanners exhibit few differences in appearance, but the innards and the capabilities vary like the contents of an encyclopedia. The optimum selection for an installation depends in part on procedures for acquiring documents. (Courtesy FileNet)

- **Manual scanning.** *Manual scanning* is the manual feeding of documents into a scanner. It is a slow process that improves verification. The utility decreases as the volume of document input increases. Yet for lower density inputs, it is still the mode of choice.

- **Batch scanning.** *Batch scanning* is when a mechanical feeder is attached to the scanner. Out of necessity, verification shifts to a greater emphasis on automation, but minor errors can multiply. This mode is probably the most economical. If documents require extensive attribute input, it can be done by personnel at workstations after acquisition.

- **FAX.** A *FAX* machine is a type of scanner located at the other end of a telephone line. The machine scans a document, compresses it, and sends it to an image system over a network. In practice, the indexing work is done at the receiving end. In that case, the senders should have their own workstations and then transmit the workups to the central location of a wide-area network.

- **Coded data.** *Coded data* composes bar codes, optically readable characters, and other patterns that are computer recognizable. The idea is to reduce manual entry of attribute data and perhaps improve verification; however, this mode usually needs forms for document input. Not all documents are created on forms, and it could be counterproductive to force this approach. Notice that the coded data mode can be combined with any of the other three modes.

The reasons why scanning is error-prone are often self-evident. Operators can overlook information on the backside of a page, skip a page, or simply fail to scan a document at all. Fortunately, error rates in practice are very low, and most corporations keep original documents for a period that ranges from one week to two months. Of the few errors that do occur, at least 99 percent of them should become apparent within this interim backup period. After that, the risks are too negligible to justify any further retention of the paper (legal requirements can mandate retention). Certainly, the residual error rate is much smaller than older methods of filing documents.

Now it is laundry list time. The options, features, and points to consider when buying scanners:

- Input mechanism/page handling
- Scan both sides of a document
- Verification capabilities
- Reduction/enlargement capability
- Size and range of input documents
- Weight, size, and "footprint"
- Noise level
- Temperature and humidity requirements
- Reliability
- Document stamping
- Bilevel, graytone, or color capability
- Resolution and range
- Voice recognition capability
- Bar codes/OCR reading
- Ability to screen/filter specific colors
- Contrast adjustment
- Output format
- Computer interface capabilities
- Amount of RAM
- Power requirements
- Operator controls/menus
- Electrical safety
- Light source/type
- Programmability
- Warranty and/or service contracts available
- Price

Too often, we take the capabilities of the human eye for granted. The eye comes with most of the preceding capabilities, and in practice it scans "images" set to the most expensive options: color, high resolution, and verification—all with minimum environmental restrictions.

To look at matters a different way, scanner prices range from $2 thousand to $50 thousand. The capabilities of the human eye would place it among the high-priced scanners. By contrast, the scanners used in image systems tend to crowd the lower end of the range because most documents consist of standard-size paper and forms that seldom pose exceptional scanning problems.

6.2 Access

Access means to view one or more documents or other images on a monitor, combined with the capability of sending the bitstream to a printer if hardcopy is needed. The choice of monitors and printers is broad enough to cover just about any conceivable requirement (FIG. 6-2). Assuming that the index and attribute logic of a system is efficient, many choices are available.

Fig. 6-2. Monitors do not vary as much as scanners, and the choice of models and features is not as critical. Nevertheless, serious mistakes in selecting monitors can negate some of the productivity gained by installing an image system.

Most monitors have zoom and reduction capabilities. Also, many monitors can rotate images and filter "noise" from the image—especially when the input requirements (for legal reasons) mandate that the image be as close as possible to the original. Still other monitors (multi-media) can display different types of images.

Screens for image systems are larger than conventional monitors and come in two basic types: portrait and landscape. The portrait type has a longer vertical dimension and is used primarily to display standard-size documents in the same size as the original. Landscape monitors, by contrast, have a longer horizontal dimension and are used to display reduced-size images and other documents or text information along side.

A few systems rely on conventional Video Graphics Array (VGA) monitors (or EGA), at least for some stations. These monitors are not practical for sustained work with standard-size image records, but they do suffice for occasional use. VGA monitors are adequate for a manager who accesses records on an ad hoc basis.

Some workstations have one (or one of each) per worker, some have one landscape-type per worker and one portrait-type for two workers, and still others share a set of monitors. The choice is usually based on frequency of accesses and the types of document images retrieved. However, in some installations, several alternatives can be equally acceptable. In short, monitors per se rarely pose any problems.

Of more interest to planners and analysts is the issue of combining acquisition with access and processing. If these tasks are to be combined, an appropriate mix of monitors (and scanners) must be determined. Once the decision is made, it would be expensive to change the setup. Accordingly, it does not hurt to prototype this element of an image system.

Printers are another matter. Their features and price ranges are even broader than scanners. Thus, the laundry list for scanners applies, with few exceptions, here also. The primary differences are that the operating functions of printers work in reverse.

Moreover, given the purpose of image processing to reduce (if not eliminate) paper documents, most organizations try to limit the paper copy to documents that must be mailed and those that are used as interim worksheets. In other words, as far as the organization is concerned, the paper will not be internally filed. When a copy must be filed, it should be added to the image folder and the original should be destroyed.

6.3 Networks

Except for the simplest desktop installations, image systems inevitably use local-area network (LAN) workstations, and most have the capability or at least the potential to transmit and receive image records over wide-area networks. In practice, roughly 80 percent of vendor systems can use Ethernet; 70 percent can use token rings; more than 60 percent can use Novells; and more than 40 percent can use 3COMs. Even when existing LANs are incompatible with a particular vendor's system, but that system has overriding advantages, it is sometimes better to go ahead with it, set up a separate network for the imaging, and use emulation to link it with the existing network. The criterion would be the amount of traffic that will flow between the two.

The chief problem with networks is the length of image records, which sometimes requires modification to the protocols and other operating software. This is more the case with wide area networks than local ones, because the former has a much lighter traffic density and the longer records have to be sliced into tiny packets. Technical note C.6 examines a few of the more salient points on this, but communication requirements rarely stymie an otherwise well-thought system.

When configuring a set-up, the last thing that needs to be considered is the network. The set-up should be designed to meet processing and records management requirements, to include transmission of records among separate sites. Whatever that set-up will be, existing network technology can accommodate it more than 99 percent of the time. The only minor exception to this approach occurs when the resolution of centralization-versus-distribution hinges on comparative costs, a point covered in section 8.3.

7

Processing and software

Algebraic symbols are used when you don't know what you are talking about.

Schoolboy response on a quiz

Traditionally, software development lags hardware technology. When image hardware first reached the commercial marketplace, however, the vendors knew that the software had to be capable of handling the obvious database functions. Experience with records management systems then revealed a lot more to do.

It is tempting to conclude that hardware technology has progressed to the point where it can meet almost any need at a reasonable price—only the software needs to be improved. That's just not true. The price of hardware needs to drop before many applications will experience significant cost savings. Next, most systems will benefit from standardization, improved wide-area network efficiency, and resolution of the legal implications of the various technologies. Still, the challenge of software looms large.

Where, then, is a good starting point? Arguably, it would be to focus on the different levels of software requirements. The old division of programming into systems software and applications software won't cut it anymore. Further, many vendors have packaged proprietary user-modifiable software, but this flexibility varies with the vendor. Therefore, the decisionmakers need to address the software load in terms of the different levels of required programs.

7.1 Processing levels

As shown in FIG. 7-1, image system programming occurs at five levels. The lower the level, the more it is likely to be part of a vendor's system and less subject to modification by users. Conversely, the higher the level, the more options become available to the user. Bear in mind that software costs are still the most expensive element in systems, both for development and maintenance costs.

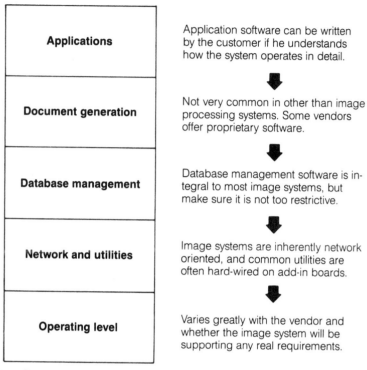

Applications	Application software can be written by the customer if he understands how the system operates in detail.
Document generation	Not very common in other than image processing systems. Some vendors offer proprietary software.
Database management	Database management software is integral to most image systems, but make sure it is not too restrictive.
Network and utilities	Image systems are inherently network oriented, and common utilities are often hard-wired on add-in boards.
Operating level	Varies greatly with the vendor and whether the image system will be supporting any real requirements.

Fig. 7-1. Image systems have five levels of software, of which the three lowest are mandatory and usually part of the vendor's package. The higher levels are helpful if the customer has the expertise and knowledge of the system.

- **Applications level.** In some systems, the applications level software is the major software element and is satellited on the lower levels. In other systems, it is inserted wherever necessary to accommodate requirements that go beyond the capability of lower levels. The latter is the prevalent mode because most image systems are oriented to automating application processing and records management rather than decision support systems. The common exception composes management reports for the system itself.

- **Document generation level.** As discussed in the next section, the document generation uses a specialized kind of software that is unique to image systems. Vendors began to offer packages for this purpose in 1990. This software is somewhat similar (but more sophisticated) to popular forms of design software coupled with a graphics variation that positions fields of data at the appropriate places on the image.

- **Database management level.** Without exception, every image system requires some form of database management software, and (as discussed in chapter 5) it is more complex than its counterpart in data processing. First, the index is usually maintained on a different medium. Second, an increase in attribute data is typical. Third, image records must often be crosslinked in more ways. This software inevitably is packaged with the image system hardware, though it can be tailored and modified by users.

- **Network and utility level.** Common network software systems are readily adapted to image processing. For the most part, boards are installed in workstations, scanners and/or printers to compress and decompress images. At the other end, operating software for the core of the image system is designed to work with a network. For similar reasons, wide-area communications do not present major problems. An image record is a bitstream like any record; once in a network, it can be routed anywhere using existing protocols.

- **Operating level.** *Operating-level software*, or what formerly was called *systems software*, is designed to work on specific hardware and is the least interchangeable of all levels. If the vendor offers a self-standing system package (or one that is designed to work primarily on one brand of computer), then the issues of operating-level software are moot. If the system is designed to operate on any computer, the customer should assure himself that all the elements are fully compatible. Unfortunately, the term *compatible* means different things to different individuals. If the vendor says he *thinks* he can develop the necessary emulation during installation to make the elements compatible, run (do not walk) to the nearest exit.

7.2 Generated documents

Paperwork causes more paperwork. Image processing has had little impact on that truism, but it has automated some of the offspring. The processing takes text material and superimposes it over a standard layout or form, which is a variation on vector imaging. So, the document can be stored in three thousand bytes, rather than in 50 thousand or 60 thousand (not counting the one-time storing of the form). When hardcopy is necessary (everyday for insurance policies), the vector image is sent to a printer, and voila, the document is in hand.

Unfortunately, not all generated documents are that simple, but a little ingenuity can reduce the workload and the storage requirements in most cases. Among these cases are: intermediate documents that must, for one reason or another, be in hardcopy while in use; modifications or extensions to existing documents (for example, zoning drawings); and documents for managing the system itself (FIG. 7-2). Other documents, such as overlays to engineering drawings and plats, are a combination of original and generated

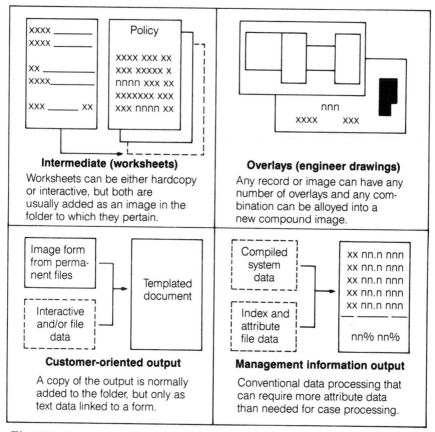

Fig. 7-2. Generated documents fall into three generic categories: intermediate, add-on, and final. Most intermediate documents are local-use worksheets. Final documents take two forms: output to customers and internal management reports.

images. Some points to note are:

- **Intermediate hardcopy worksheets.** Worksheets are common to most application-oriented operations, and also to many other types. Because the eye and hand is quicker than the keyboard and mouse, the use of paper is still more efficient. Hardcopies can be generated by a printer when necessary or mass-printed supplies can be kept on hand—whichever is the most economical in the long run. The choice is less important than ensuring that the worksheet is imaged into the electronic folder to which it pertains.

- **Output documents.** Insurance policies and letters of transmittal are common examples of output documents, although hundreds more exist. Most output documents are computer generated with a minimum of additional input information and are not normally stored as image records. Instead, the necessary information is stored in a text format with linkage data. Then, it is superimposed over the appropriate form image.

- **Systems management reports.** These reports are computer generated from statistical data compiled from acquisitions and access. Each report can be as simple or comprehensive as the customer wants it. They can include detailed information on who accessed what or present only the most-generalized data summations.

- **Engineering overlays.** This is perhaps the most fascinating type of image work, especially for cartography. A basic image of the terrain, area, or zone is developed and is used as a baseline for specialized images. For example, a city management system would have overlays for different utilities, zoning restrictions, voting districts, and so forth. Any combination of these overlays can be compiled and printed as a single document. Thus, one edition might depict a correlation of electric and gas lines, another of zoning versus tax rates, and still another for construction permits and existing tax rates. This technique is also useful for blueprints, for certain types of scientific and medical research, and even for publishing.

7.3 Vendor products

Many vendors offer software packages. Sometimes the names of these packages refer just to software, and sometimes it refers to a larger system of which the software is an integral part. Logically, the packages are similar, but seldom interchangeable, and some are more flexible than others. Lastly, some of the modifications require a detailed knowledge of the hardware and lower-order operating systems. Until customers become experts with that hardware, some of the modifications should be done by the vendor.

Theoretically, the most difficult problem with vendor software is ensuring that the differences and similarities are understood. In practice, the burden imposed on management is to convince themselves that the selected vendor can meet the requirements. Anything that can be reduced to logic can be programmed, and any vendor can theoretically adapt its software to meet any requirement. The questions are: how long will it take, what is the cost, and how easy will it be to make modifications later? To answer these questions, the customer must have a firm idea of: the magnitude of records that will be stored, the processing requirements (including interfaces with other databases), and any documentation generation requirements. Once these answers are known, a good vendor will indicate how its software can be used to meet higher level requirements, and how its lower level software will support the system.

Thus, a detailed description of each vendor's software in this book would probably be inappropriate and would become outdated within six months. The brief descriptions provided here are intended only as an orientation and are drawn mostly from descriptive references provided by the vendors.

- **FileNet's WorkFlo.** This software has evolved over five years, and it therefore lacks the appearance of an integrated package created with the benefit of hindsight. Nevertheless, the features added subsequently work just as well as if they had been developed as part of the original package. The basic software tailors screen appearances, controls the flow of documents, sets and adjusts priorities, juggles multiple processing actions, and generates management reports. WorkFlo Queue Services extends the processing to multiple platforms and CDP (compound document software) generates multi-media documents. WorkFlo Sentinel Service logs errors and performs numerous systems checks. FileNet also provides COLD and COM software. Some of the software offered by other vendors was developed under license to FileNet.

- **Wang Integrated Image System.** Though Wang calls their system integrated, like FileNet, it consists of a basic package and optional add-ons. Basic Image Support Package performs functions similar to FileNet's WorkFlo, but it is more limited. The advantage is its low entry price (a benefit for very small systems). It also lends itself to integration with user-programmed software in Assembler, Fortran 77, Cobol, C, and PL1. Finally, users can select from a wide range of specialized software add-ons. An example of a specialized add-on is High Volume Scanning Software, an important contribution to the industry. Document acquisition is error prone, and as the need for batch scanning rises in popularity, this kind of software will rise in importance and undoubtedly encourage competitors to write similar packages.

- **DECimage.** Digital Equipment Corporation's DECimage takes a slightly different approach than FileNet or Wang. It consists of a number of software building blocks: Image Input Services, Storage Manager, Image Display Service, and Image Services Library. The last item, of course, accommodates customer-written subroutines (or subroutines that DEC writes for a customer under contract).

- **InfoImage (Unisys).** Unisys takes a product-family approach. The generalized package is InfoImage Folder (intended for business document and file folder applications). Most of its functions are common to all image systems. But it's add-ons focus on specific applications, for example: InfoImage IIPS (for high-speed payment processing) and InfoImage EDMS (for large-format technical documents). Apparently, the strategy of Unisys is to stay in the commercial mainstream and to zero in on specialized markets, where specialized software works more efficiently.

- **IBM's ImagePlus.** In contrast to other vendors, IBM does not emphasize software per se. What it markets is ImagePlus, a strongly related family of elements designed to be satellited on various IBM computers and on scanners, printers and other peripherals from a wide range of manufacturers. Thus, its software is too integral to its system to warrant a spotlight. The special needs of each customer are programmed as necessary, sometimes by way of standing subcontractors. As business builds however, they will develop a rich library from which to draw.

Many other vendors have entered the image software market, some with complete packages, others with specialized add-ons, and still others on a custom programming basis. Space limitations prevent descriptions for each vendor and the author apologizes that if by highlighting these five vendors that any injustice has been done to the others.

Part III

Issues

Image processing has raised a host of issues, not the least of which is the debate on optical disk technology versus micrographics (FIG. III-1). Depending on the speaker's point of view, image processing either will doom the latter to obsolescence or it will give it new life. Accordingly, some vendors have little patience for microforms and others have engineered efficient technology to integrate the two.

Additional issues include centralization versus distribution, integration trade-offs, standardization, several security concerns exacerbated by the nature of image records, the acceptability of optical disk images as evidence in legal proceedings, and the potential for massive copyright violations. Not every installation faces all of these issues, but at least some of them are bound to crop up in every project and system.

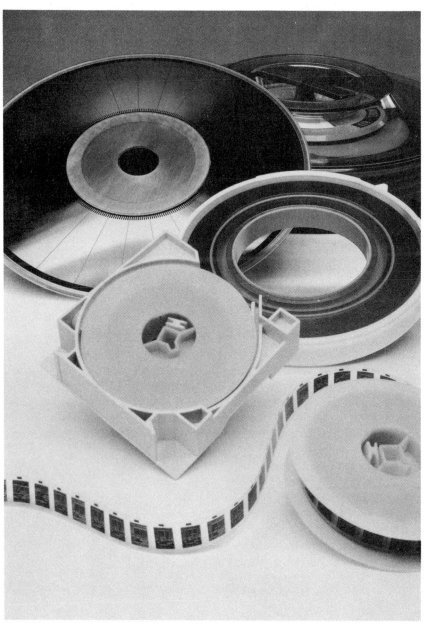

Fig. III-1. A variety of storage formats for image processing. (Courtesy Eastman Kodak)

8

Wherewithal

I never saw an instance of one of two
disputants convincing the other by argument.
I have seen many, on their getting warm,
becoming rude and shooting one another.

Thomas Jefferson

The wherewithal of image technology forces many issues, some from the viewpoint of each installation, others primarily from the perspective of vendors, and still others that sweep the landscape of all forms of automated processing. When it comes to hardware, most of these issues tend to focus on the individual customer, especially when the intended projects increase in size.

Of these hardware-oriented issues, the choice of storage techniques is the most prevalent. Although the optical disk is the medium of choice, much is to be said for microforms and optical tape (FIG. 8-1). What's more, professionals in the imaging processing field are coming to recognize that these alternatives are more complementary than antagonistic. The next issue, integration, presents a greater challenge. Although two or more image systems can be integrated, the concept of alloying data and images runs headlong into a logical impasse. Data is processed; images are viewed.

The third issue is somewhat related to the second—deciding between centralized and distributed image processing. If the system is installed at multiple sites, existing data processing might benefit from a centralized system, whereas the economics of imaging could favor distributive processing. All three of these issues then help frame the fourth: should the organization buy imaging now or later?

8.1 Storage media

Some observers regard image processing and the optical disk as essentially synonymous, but that isn't the case. At least two other options rate attention, and as mentioned above, both are gaining increasing respectability:

- **Optical tape.** A single reel of optical tape that is essentially the same size as a standard reel of magnetic tape can hold the same amount of information as a jukebox that is as big as a true cord of wood. It costs only a small fraction of the equivalent storage capacity on optical disks, and the driver is much less expensive than jukeboxes. At least one vendor offers the hardware for this option under $200,000 and they report that an entire tape can be scanned in less than a minute.

• **Microforms.** Microfilm has been in use since the 1920s. It is available in three forms: *microfilm, microfiche,* and *aperture cards.* The first two are well known. An aperture card consists of a frame of microfilm (usually 35mm) mounted in a punch card or its equivalent and it is used primarily for engineering drawings and similar materials. Directly readable information is printed on the carrier card.

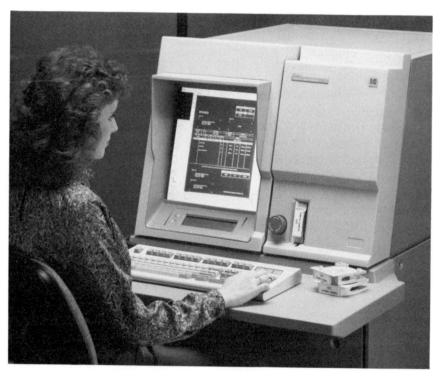

Fig. 8-1. Although optical disks outpace microfilm in growth percentages, the latter is still the leader in absolute terms. Its advantages are low cost, durability, and now the capability of being integrated with image systems. (Courtesy Eastman Kodak)

It's fair to assume that organizations with a heavy investment in microform technology will continue to use it unless optical disk systems would yield a major savings. A more relevant criterion is the speed of access. Here, on-line optical disks win hands down. Thus, the practical criterion becomes: at what point do reduced access requirements justify the economy of the alternatives? The question has a different answer for each application: security backup, inactive records, and backfile conversion.

- **Security backup.** The alternatives are ideal for backup purposes, except when the backup must be pressed into service at a moment's notice. Both media are less expensive than optical disks, and the technology exists to write scanned images directly to optical disks (COLD— Computer Output to Laser Disks) and to microform (COM—Computer Output to Microforms). Moreover, Eastman Kodak is working on a scanner that will combine COLD and COM.

- **Inactive records.** If active records are written on WORM disks, it makes little sense to transfer them later to another medium—especially if they are already on backup. If the records are written to rewritable disks, however, the advantages are obvious—again providing that no permanent backup already exists.

- **Backfile conversion.** The subject of *backfile conversion* is covered in technical note C.7. Backfiles consist of both active and inactive paper records. Active records, for the most part, would require the same medium as newly acquired ones, but the same is not necessarily true for inactive records. In that case, no image records would exist in any form, and therefore the alternative mediums would probably be attractive.

8.2 Integration

Integration means many things to many people, even in the tight world of computer science. The central idea is to put the concept of interior lines (section 2.4) into practice, so that information and data from different sources can be easily and momentarily consolidated in order to support decisionmaking. Those decisions can range from loan approvals to changing the strategic direction of a company. With respect to image processing, the lower-order types will dominate more so than in data processing. The exception occurs when existing manual procedures are so cumbersome that they cannot be used to compile necessary statistical information for higher level decisions. Case example B.2 presents such a situation. To continue with the general subject of integration, three forms exist (FIG. 8-2):

- **Merger.** A *merger* alloys different automated systems into one, so that users accept the result as singular. A common analogy is a blender, but a more accurate one would be in an old-fashioned hardware store. You bring in a problem, and the proprietor leads you to various shelves until he has assembled the necessary items for you to solve it.

- **Interface.** An *interface* links systems without attempting to eliminate their respective identities. The CIRRUS network and the airlines reservations systems are excellent examples of interface integration, and any wide-area network can be used to interface any number of image systems. From the perspective of a network, an image record is just another bitstream. However, when the sender and receiver have different systems, that bitstream must be processed through at least one emulation stage.

- **Local standardization.** A standardized approach is when identical or so-called fully compatible equipment is used in all systems that are maintained by an organization. Take the expression "fully compatible" with the proverbial grain of salt, although the great progress in image technology standardization will in time obviate the need for that caution. The idea is to facilitate other forms of integration, but in some cases, the effect is to create one by default.

	Concept	Significance for image systems
Mergers	To alloy all or parts of separate systems so that the result gives at least the appearance of being a single entity to users. Mergers can take any one of three subforms.	• Total mergers are impractical • Database mergers, at least in terms of access, have become increasingly common. • Extract mergers, beyond management of the system itself, are specialized applications.
Interfaces	An interface opens channels of communication between or among two or more systems that retain their separate identities.	• The simplest form merely transmits bitstreams between systems as needed. • More complex interfaces approach the database subform of a merger integration.
Local standardizations	This form makes all elements of targeted systems identical or fully compatible. The trend to vendor standardization makes this easier.	• The result may or may not be an integration, but if not, the effect will facilitate another form of integration, especially a database merger and complex interfaces.

Fig. 8-2. Integration can take many forms and can operate at many levels, but the three basic forms are: merging existing systems into one, interfacing essentially independent data and systems, and standardizing locally, which also lowers operating costs.

The merger type of integration has three variations. Their applications depend on whether the object is to integrate two or more image processing elements or to merge image and data processing:

- **Synthesis.** A synthesis alloys separate systems to the point where the members are no longer identifiable as manageable entities. The result is equivalent to adding features to an existing system.

- **Database.** A database merger is a logical synthesis in the sense that all targeted information (data or image) is indexed so that users can access any or all of it from any station—as if it was all stored in one place.

- **Extract.** This form of merger merely extracts critical information from several sources and puts the copies into one system.

So much for theory. The practice of integration is another matter. The problem is that raster image records and conventional databases are fundamentally incompatible. The former is intended for human viewing, as if it was still on paper. The other is intended for processing, with the results of that processing usually displayed on one medium or another. Thus, what is usually meant by integration in an image system is one of three situations:

- **Common database.** A true merger of physical wherewithal would probably be counterproductive. At the present time, the only way to do this would be to replace most of the hardware and software. The more practical option is to merge separate databases. This does not mandate a physical consolidation, only a logical one. So, index data for each record would be unique no matter where it resides. Moreover, any user in the system could enter that index data and retrieve any record stored in any other location.

- **Interfaced database.** This situation is similar in appearance and effect to a common database, but it does not require that the same imaging technology be used at each location. Rather, hardware and/or software emulations can translate requests and bitstreams so that the various stations can communicate. This system is slower and would probably encounter some logical disconnects from time to time. However, if existing systems were not designed with a merged database in mind, it is a practical alternative.

- **Expandability.** The term *integration* is sometimes misused to mean that when an image system is to be expanded, the new elements should work well with the existing ones. The original set-up should be designed with that idea in mind. It would have to be configured as a full-size system and then only the initial components would be installed.

Anything less than this design would probably incur major problems when it comes time to hook them up. Of course, using standardized elements of hardware, networks, and software packages will facilitate the expansion immensely.

Superintending the issue of integrations is the matter of subjective motivation versus compelling necessity. The human tendency is to integrate for the sake of integration, no matter the cost. The better approach is determine what information should be integrated and what the trade-off is between cost and increased interior lines.

8.3 Centralization versus distribution

If "to be or not to be" was the stumper for Hamlet, centralized or distributed processing is the quandary for image systems. Figure 8-3 depicts the key advantages of each, but the relative weight of those advantages varies too much with specific installations to be a useful guide. Much depends on the density of transmission, which would result from using one option or the other, and the compatibility of the ideal set-up with existing systems. Moreover, emerging technology will tend to favor increased centralization, but not necessarily for the most active records at local sites.

Accordingly, each of the factors depicted in FIG. 8-3 warrants further discussion:

- **Logical integrity and relatability.** A centralized system offers the best opportunity to ensure that data, information, and records that are logically related remain in that state within the system. Whenever separate indexes are maintained in separate locations, the risk is that they will become distended with respect to each other (a problem discussed in more detail in section 10.2). But if the separate databases have little in common, except to compile statistical data derived from the separate sites, then the logical integrity issue becomes moot.

- **Security.** In theory, distributive processing favors security, because no single point of catastrophic failure exists. But if any element in a distributed system is critical to the whole, that advantage is nullified. Also, the term *failure* needs to be defined. Does it mean the destruction of optical disks? Of optical disk drivers? A temporary shutdown of the system?

- **Facilitation of local use.** The effect of centralizing systems where distant users depend on them is to impose a mechanical bureaucracy between what needs to be done and the material essential to do it. Predictably, most requirements that emanate at the central site will take priority, and higher level managers might use this resource to micromanage subordinate divisions.

- **Costs.** Distributive processing is less expensive when traffic among the stations is minimal, and more expensive when the contrary prevails. However, this statement is oversimplified. The cost picture is actually a function that varies with the degree of centralization imposed on a particular set of processing requirements.

- **Integration.** The centralization-versus-distribution issue takes a turn for the worse when existing data processing leans in one direction and image processing the opposite. For starters, use of existing wide-area networks could be overloaded. The attempt to integrate various databases by way of a consolidated index could be a monumental undertaking. Further, once an election is made to use one or the other mode, and later circumstances favor a change, the existing set-ups might not easily accommodate it.

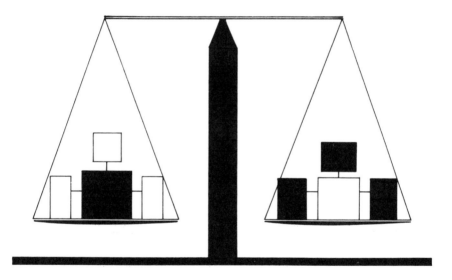

Favoring centralization

- Logical integrity

- Maximum relatability

Favoring distribution

- Aversion of disasters

- Local use facilitated

Factors that vary with the situation

- Integration with existing systems

- Comparative costs of alternatives

Fig. 8-3. The degree to which an image system should be centralized, rather than distributed, depends on many factors. Moreover, as emerging technology comes on the market and the system expands, the weight of the factors changes.

8.4 Buying now or later

On the question of buying now or later, vendors will tend to advocate the former. The stated reason is typically to gain strategic advantage before competitors do. The savings that might accrue by waiting for prices to drop (the reasoning continues) could be wiped out by failing to harness that advantage as soon as possible or that cost savings over the next few years will more than compensate for the higher installation price. In some cases, this reasoning might be correct and in others not so correct. If the need for an image system is compelling or if it will generate indisputable major cost savings, the issue is moot. Buy now. If otherwise, consider these factors:

- **Capabilities.** Image processing capabilities will improve markedly over the next five years, and the fruits of standardization will take root. Further, a variety of custom-developed programs will undoubtedly be consolidated as the equivalent of productivity software and marketed for a much lower price. The work on neural optical character recognition (of handwriting) might not be available any time soon, but the use of bar codes and regular OCR on forms will progress to the point where document acquisition will be far simpler. To go any further than this would be pure speculation.

- **Costs.** The cost and return-on-investment picture can be drawn in many ways, favorable or unfavorable, depending on the values plugged in. What is certain is that the cost of imaging systems will drop over the next five years; or the equivalent, the same dollar will buy more system. This reduction in cost could more than offset the interim savings.

- **Subjectivity of the bandwagon syndrome.** Perhaps the worst reason for adapting any technology is that "everybody else is doing it," the corporate equivalent of "keeping up with the Joneses." There is no logical dealing with this mindset. If a system is decided upon under questionable need, the only thing subordinates can do is make the best of it, and concentrate on choosing one that will work best under a broad range of requirements.

9

Standardization

The shop seemed to be full of all manner
of curious things—but the oddest part of it
was that, whenever she looked hard at any shelf,
to make out exactly what it had on it,
that particular shelf was always quite empty,
though the others 'round about it were as crowded
as they could hold. "Things flow about so here!"
she said at last in a plaintive tone.

Through the Looking Glass by
Lewis Carroll (Charles Dodgson)

Standardization means following agreed-upon methods for doing things. Image processing standardization is proceeding much faster than it has been in the data processing. Moreover, the endeavor encompasses virtually every aspect of image processing except one—the correct term for image processing itself.

Ten of the more popular contenders are: electronic imaging, information and image management, document processing, document image processing, document imaging, electronic document management, computer document management, optical information systems, optical disk systems, and of course, image processing. In all fairness, most of these terms and expressions have discrete definitions; therefore, no one term can accommodate all of the nuances. This situation is no different than exists on the other side of the fence: data processing, automated data processing, electronic data processing, automated processing, automated systems, and whatever. Fortunately, the term *image processing* itself has taken on a generic mantle, so it was used for the title of this book.

9.1 Standardization environment

In the United States, the leadership role for standardization is almost entirely under the Association for Information and Image Management (AIIM), although the final approval is given by the American National Standards Institute (ANSI) Board of Standards Review. Internationally, standardization comes under the Organization of International Standards (ISO). AIIM, through ANSI, participates in the work of ISO. Notice, however, that international acceptance of a proposed standard is a complex task—more so for image processing than for micrographics. Therefore, in practice the AIIM concentrates on U.S. standards.

According to AIIM publications, the process is straightforward and averages between two-and-one-half and three years. It follows this path:

- A group proposes an idea to the AIIM Standards Board.
- If voted on favorably, the board assigns it to a standing committee.
- If no appropriate committee exists, a new one forms (rare).
- A subcommittee (drafting group) prepares a draft standard.
- The committee votes on it.
- If necessary, the draft is revised.
- Once approved by the committee, the Standards Board votes on it.
- If approved, the draft goes to the AIIM membership, to the National Standards Council (NSC) and to ANSI for public review, all concurrently.
- The results are compiled and sent to the ANSI review board.
- If approved by ANSI (the main criterion is that due process was followed), ANSI provides an approval date.

Standards, of course, are not law. Compliance is voluntary, but within a short time vendors need to justify any variance to savvy customers. Note also that ANSI standards exist at two levels: standards and standard recommended practices. The latter recognizes the need for a slightly more flexible approach than is permitted by a standard. AIIM also produces technical reports on matters that need a push toward standardization, but where the field is still too young or volatile to secure the necessary agreement to lead to a formal standard.

The AIIM Standards Board consists of 12 volunteers who are representative of the various section of vendors and users from the micrographic and electronic imaging technologies. It is chaired by the AIIM Director of Standards and Technology as an exception to the general practice that other AIIM committees are chaired by volunteers. The reason is that the follow-up work is too extensive to impose on a volunteer.

Further, to preclude even the appearance of parochialism, this board works with a substantial number of other organizations, including:

ARMM	Association of Reprographic Manufactures and Materials
GSA	General Services Administration
NAGARA	National Association of Government Archives and Records Administrators
NAPM	National Association of Photographic Manufacturers
NCSC	National Center for State Courts

NISO   National Information Standards Organization
RLG   Research Libraries Group
SAA   Society of American Archivists
SLA   Special Libraries Association
SPSE   Society for Image Science and Technology

In addition, AIIM works closely with the Department of Defense (DoD) Computer-aided Acquisition and Logistic Support (CALS) program. One of the goals of CALS (which is still evolving) is to impose standard procedures on documentation and other records related to government contracts and procurement. With the advent of image processing, these procedures often overlap with the standardization process for technical matters, and therefore poses the risk of conflict. That risk has been reduced by taking the initiative to coordinate standardization work with the DoD agencies responsible for CALS.

Also the open architectural environment among most image processing vendors causes an effect. No one vendor dominates the field; however, if Eastman Kodak had teamed up with IBM rather than DEC, it might have been a different story. Moreover, because very few vendors are in a position to manufacture all the components in imaging systems, it is to their advantage to push for standards.

A supporting reason for this trend, perhaps the strongest one, is that image processing burst on the market suddenly because of its inherent ability to draw together and adapt many proven technologies from different vendors. The central technical contribution of FileNet was the large-scale optical disk library—the jukebox. Local-area networks had long since proven themselves. The logic of the relational database system was well established, as was the scanner and compression algorithm derived from the familiar fax machine. The optical disk was also a proven technology, albeit first in CD-ROM form.

9.2 Problems besetting standardization

Perhaps the best way to perceive standardization is to consider the optical disk. It always looks simple, but it represents, if not entails, more than a dozen problems for standardization.

For starters, consider size. The three common sizes are 5.25-inch, 12-inch, and 14-inch disks (FIG. 9-1). Something is to be said for having at least two sizes, the smaller one for very small systems (primarily an outgrowth of the CD-ROM industry). The introduction of the 14-inch size, however, grated on the nerves of those who were working hard on standardization. It will not likely change.

Next is the matter of recording technology. Admittedly, the fact that these disks are available in WORM and rewritable forms is not an area of concern for standardization. Some requirements benefit from the more permanent storage

Fig. 9-1. The optical disk appears to be a unifying idea for image processing—virtually all image systems use them. Unfortunately, like magnetic storage disks in data processing, dozens of variations exist among vendors. (Courtesy Eastman Kodak).

of the former, but economics dictate using the latter in other situations. What of the different recording techniques for each? These technologies are discussed in technical note C.4, but the point here is that they are not readily interchangeable. These technologies probably will not become interchangeable, except possibly in the drawn-out heat of competition. Many of these alternative technologies are already in widespread use.

Next come the issues of density, number of tracks, thickness, and so forth. For the most part, these items are also beyond the reach of standardization. The idea of progress is to shoehorn more and more material into less and less space. Competition among manufacturers leaves no time to even attempt to standardize this area, except perhaps for the nomenclature and the physical label on a disk.

So much for physical characteristics. What about formatting and directories? Here again, the goal of standardization is at the mercy of the different products (drivers) already in widespread use. This situation is not much different from what occurs in data processing, except for the ubiquitous IBM-compatible micros.

All right, so this is beyond practical reach. What about record formats, the bitstream of the stored record? Here some real progress is possible, primarily because of the industry-wide acceptance of the CCITT standard for compression algorithms. Although this standard is not quite as uniform in practice as one might like to think, the effort to close the gap is vigorous. Compression algorithms for picture-oriented images are another matter, but the work being done by the Joint Photograph Experts Group (JPEG) promises a standard (perhaps within three years).

Next comes the criteria for scanning images and for displaying them afterwards. Here again, standardization can only play a passive role. This technology can be developed and proclaimed (quality control checks and samples for example), but they cannot be imposed on vendors. And when it comes to spectral image types, the door closes tighter. Different requirements need different techniques, and competition searches for more economical ways to pack more finely resolved images into tighter spaces. Finally, none of this even begins to address differences in software and in index algorithms that are critical to the integration of systems and the exchange of information.

To make matters even worse, the government (especially the Department of Defense) attempts to impose certain standards for the submission and files management of documents—for example, the Computer-aided Acquisition and Logistics Support (CALS) program. Those criteria are not always aligned with ongoing work in standardization. Moreover, many federal (and state) requests for proposals bypass existing standards. In fine, standardization has a tough row to hoe.

9.3 Some examples of standardization work

The first EIM standard developed by an AIIM committee was *MS44, the Recommended Practice for Quality Control of Image Scanners*. More than 30 organizations contributed to this standard and more than 2,000 copies of it have been distributed. It includes procedures for testing scanners, although test objects, such as the IEEE Facsimile Test Chart and the AIIM Scanner Target, are sold separately.

Another standard in progress is *Electronic Imaging Output*, which covers printers and display devices for paper sizes up to 11×17 inches and resolutions up to 400 pixels per inch. The same committee also wrote a report on *tiling*. Tiling subdivides an image record into blocks, somewhat similar to subdividing a bitstream into packets for transmission. Without it, existing workstation hardware would have a hard time managing and displaying images.

Other committees are producing guidelines for developing requests for proposals for image processing systems. If much of the technology is beyond the reach of true standardization, at least written communications can eliminate or at least reduce the ambiguities. Still other committees are working on data interchange standards (in conjunction with the organizations that have primary responsibility for communications standards), life expectancy test methods, image marking and tagging, presentation formats, disk formats and file structure (despite existing practices), and refinement of the CCITT T.6 Group 4 compression algorithm.

As mentioned previously, this compression algorithm was developed to solve a major compatibility problem for transmitting images between FAX machines. The problem was that the published standard was somewhat ambiguous, especially on the algorithm parameters. As a result, records purported as being "compressed according to the standard" are not always decompressible on other machines without software emulation.

This problem is very troublesome because different systems use different values for the parameters. If only two different sets of values are used, then only one emulation (if it works in both directions) is required. If three are used, the number of emulators rises to three. At five, ten emulators are necessary to cover all the bases.

9.4 Significance for managers

Any time that technical standardization evolves among vigorous competitors without the slightest hint of price fixing, customers are bound to obtain more useful products at a good price. But that advantage does not apply to existing systems. Moreover, existing systems could require expensive retrofitting.

In practical terms, it means that when projecting a new system, it benefits planners to assess the trends in standardization and opt for vendors who are leaning in that direction. This is especially true for large systems or units that will be integrated eventually, unless compelling economic reasons suggest a different course of action.

Beyond that, planners should consider using common or at least compatible hardware and software (especially on the route from the scanner to the object record on the disk) and on the indexing and attribute logic used to retrieve and work with those images. To a major extent, vendor packages ensure this. Unfortunately, this is not necessarily the case with value-added vendors (who are a cross between a consultant and a major contractor). In these situations, the potential for long-term savings can slip by in order to meet a deadline or some "here-and-now" requirement.

In summation, image systems can be made to work without regard to standardization, but most of these will be more expensive and less productive. It simply pays to buy parts that fit together well.

10

Security

Please pardon my ignorance;
this is the first time I've been beheaded.

Alexander Blackwell, 1747 on
being told he had put his head
on the block the wrong way

Commercial image processing is too new to have experienced the same range of security problems that occur in data processing. Unfortunately, all of the security problems that plague data processing also plague image processing. Worse yet, some formerly manageable problems intensify in image processing.

The three well-known security problems associated with all forms of automated processing are: protection from physical damage, reduction of logical damage and input errors, and control of unauthorized access—irrespective of the use to which the information gained is put.

The special problems with image systems stem from three sources: the length of time over which records are kept, the sheer mass of those records, and the accessibility to a much larger number of personnel who have no specialized training in computer science. If all documentation was recorded in an image system and if ten times more personnel had access to it than the data processing records, then 200 times the potential for problems would exist. That spells trouble, at least potentially, and 90 percent of all security measures aim at preventing or reducing the effects of potential trouble.

10.1 Physical loss or damage

Catastrophes are rare in data processing, and they will likely remain equally rare in image processing. Whatever measures are used to prevent this level of damage will probably work equally well for both types of systems. Of more importance, however, are the slew of minor dysfunctions that affect, and infect, systems. For data processing, these include head crashes, accidental degaussing, lost tapes, breakdown of hardware or networks, or any of 20 other sources and irritants.

Fortunately, optical disks are inherently more stable than magnetic media. Head crashes are all but impossible; the light source is one thousand times further away from the surface than a magnetic head. And accidental degaussing is also impossible, except for the equivalent problem with rewritable disks (even then the risk is lower). Further, optical disks, especially the WORM type, are not as likely to be lost. Active records are kept in jukeboxes; inactive records are kept in secure rooms and not reused for other purposes.

The higher number of users does not present any unusual problems either. No matter how many individuals use the system, access to the physical location of the disks will almost always be restricted to a few qualified operators and their supervisors. The only exception would be a desktop system or stand-alone system where the users are responsible for their own disks. In that case, disks could easily be mislaid or stolen.

This leaves the problem of intentional manipulation of the data on the disk, noting that records are often kept for seven or more years, and perhaps indefinitely. So far, major offenses of this nature have not surfaced in the trade journals, but the potential is real, both for WORM and rewritable disks. In the case of WORM, the information on disk can be obliterated by writing over the unwritten part of the recording surface. A more sophisticated hacker could modify a record by selectively writing over the untouched surface areas or by adding additional forged "documents" if any space remains (see FIG. 10-1).

A popular technique to control this problem combines the logic of hashing and the parity bit on magnetic tape. A *hash* is a number calculated from data in the key field of a record and it is used to designate the physical location of the record for random access storage. The parity bit signals if the number of the remaining eight bits turned on within its sector is even or odd.

In the case of optical disks, the pattern of writing on a record area is used to calculate a number, a hash, which is then also written into that record in a designated location. Changing the hash to correspond with the illicit additions to the record is a near mathematical impossibility. This procedure would not stop the culprit, but the change would be detected.

Unfortunately, the indexing system used for image records is usually kept on magnetic storage and is subject to immediate and total loss—as all magneti-cally stored data is. This is the weak point in image processing; therefore, backup measures are indispensable. These measures are not necessarily costly, but they must be updated continuously.

10.2 Logical loss and input errors

Erroneous data can be as troublesome as missing data, especially if the former is believed to be correct. That is, if data is missing or obviously has been tampered with, corrective actions must be taken. That is not the case for the latter. And image processing is especially susceptible to this form of error. The much larger number of records, in the absence of strict verification, is prone to an increase in input errors.

In addition, the longer periods over which records are kept subjects them to what is called *data decay* (FIG. 10-2). In data processing systems, data decay

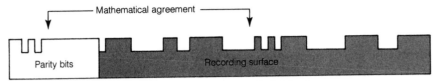

Legitimate write on an optical disk

The bitstream representing a document, compressed or uncompressed, is recorded by way of physical or chemical change to a small area on the recording surface of an optical disk. From the pattern of these marks a number is calculated—a hash—and recorded in a parity area. The logic of this hash is designed to make use of the physical geometry of the record data—position as well as amount

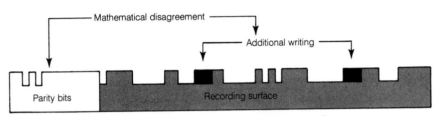

Unauthorized modification of an existing record

An image record can be modified by marking areas previously left smooth. It is difficult but not impossible to have this modification make logical sense, but even when it does it will no longer agree with the parity information.

Fig. 10-1. Optical disks are not quite as permanent as advertised. All bit patterns are recorded by modifying the recording surface, similar to magnetizing bits of ferrous material. The untouched surface can be subsequently modified.

refers to the magnetism on random bits wearing off (or uncharged bits being magnetized from stray sources). Technically, this definition also applies to image processing, but it focuses on the index. It also describes the logical "decay" of the index over time. Thus, it could become more difficult to locate older records.

By way of analogy, consider the young married couple. If careful, they will keep records on all important financial matters and will be able to find them quickly. Yet 30 years and five houses later, the situation can change. Let us say that they roll over the capital gain on their current house into the price of a new one that is priced higher than the net selling price. It's perfectly legal when all criteria are met; but if audited, they had better be prepared to substantiate the 30-year history of their housing capital costs. If not, they could be stuck with a bigger tax bill when it comes time to take advantage of the one-time nontaxable gain on their primary home. Data decay acts the same way in long-term storage systems.

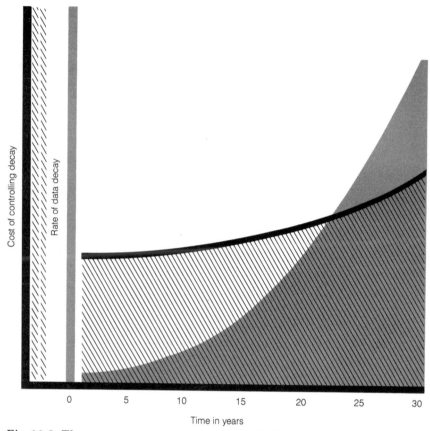

Fig. 10-2. The power curves of data decay. Accessibility in an image system decays at an exponential rate and so does the cost of containing it. On the other hand, accesses for aging records also decay at a similar rate. The intersection varies with each system, but it will occur.

Once a paper document is stored, it will more than likely retain the same index number and be kept with others in its class. The paper will not transform, nor will it be copied onto other sheets. Not so with image records. They can be reconsolidated on other disks or copied to alternative storage media (microfilm or optical tape). Also, the drivers and software that read the disks could become outdated and be difficult to keep in good repair. The favorable aspect of this unfortunate phenomenon is that as most records age, the accesses rapidly decrease. True, legal cases and deed records are some notable exceptions. Yet, only a small fraction of all documents come under these exceptions. The overwhelming bulk of them become inactive de facto after no more than three years, and in most cases they can be destroyed after seven.

The other common exception might be called *cumulative records*, such as personnel folders of career personnel. Documents in these folders become out-dated, but if they remain linked in the same folder, the data decay problem is moot.

What then should be done? What is the trade-off between a major effort to ensure that all indexes to records are current and immediately usable versus living with the consequences of decaying data? Figure 10-2 illustrates the trade-off point in terms of the intersection of cost and decay. But where that point falls will vary with the installation. Empirical data is rare this early in the development of image technology, but it is safe to assume that the expenses of controlling data decay rise exponentially with age, and that the need for access decreases also at an exponential rate.

Image processing offers two general methods of input verification: electronic and visual. Most systems employ a mixture of both. The document image is the audit trail, and to keep the original paper, unless required by law or other compelling necessity, would largely defeat the economy of the system. Or to keep the original paper past an interim period to resolve any input or scanning errors would be a mistake. Accordingly, the verification procedures must usually be tighter than when using data processing systems.

Electronic verification systems are typically built into scanners. Some can rescan each image twice and then compare the bitstreams. Others compute the record length and compare it to standard ranges for the type of document signaled by the indexing information (which might be in the form of a bar code or an OCR). The number of variations is limitless, and the verification can be set to check every document or only a sample, or different samples for different forms or types of documents.

Manual verification, by contrast, has an operator compare the images on screen with the physical documents (the images are held in temporary storage until the verification is complete). This verification process can be reduced to a set of check points or it can be more informal. The process might be required for all documents, for just a sample, or maybe exhaustive checks on a sample and cursory checks on others. Again, there is no limit to the options.

But, how much verification is necessary? Enough to keep the error rate below the set criterion. Virtually all errors are caught within the first 60 days in the life cycle of an image record, if they are caught at all. Most of these fall into two categories: a missing page (commonly the obverse side of the physical page) or incorrect index/attribute data. Many companies try to keep this error rate below 0.2 or 0.3 percent (two or three out of every 1000 documents, not pages). Any attempt to reduce the rate further is likely to be counterproductive.

So, in the absence of permanent-audit-trail procedures, should the verification process itself be documented and every detected error be documented to prove the effectiveness of the procedures? The answer depends on the extent to which the documents will be or could be used in court proceedings or to support major financial transactions.

10.3 Unauthorized access

As previewed in section 4.6, the massing of information in one system that is subject to instant access is an invitation to abuse. This abuse could be practiced by authorized users who exceed their authority or by unauthorized users under any circumstances. It does not matter if the data is left intact or destroyed, the access itself is abuse. Any destruction, incidental or intentional, lists under the heading of physical damage.

Any number of measures can be instituted to control this problem, from complex passwords to a complete recording of every access to every record by every user, or from restricted access to certain ranges of values within index fields. Again, the extent to which measures are invoked should be relative to the consequences of failing to curtail the practice. Any obstacle can be breached by a determined individual and hackers are sometimes both determined and equipped with mental genius. But what are the consequences of unauthorized access?

The last point to be discussed here is the familiar virus and worm problem. These electronic imps can work their way into any computer system and wreak havoc, usually by overwriting or erasing existing data. In image systems, the indexing files are an obvious target. Optical disks are also targets because the information can be nullified by writing on the unused sectors. The way to prevent the latter would be with a hard-wired operating system that would prevent writing on any sector of a disk after it first had been written. Just how paranoid is all this concern? About the same as similar statements made by other writers up until the day before the InfoNet case. Enough said.

11
Legal issues

It is entirely easy to settle any question if only one principle is involved. But the hang of it is that most questions—all questions that are difficult—have a conflict of at least two so-called principles.

Felix Frankfurter

Every vendor admits that acceptability of image records as evidence in court has been an issue, but most of them suggest it is being resolved favorably and should present no problem (except in isolated cases). This outlook is somewhat like the scene in the James Bond movie *Live and Let Die*. The indefatigable hero has been placed on a tiny concrete island surrounded by a pond of hungry crocodiles. He escapes to the shore by walking on their heads.

And so it is with image processing. The outlook is blithely optimistic, but ample opportunity exists for the crocodiles (plaintiffs and their attorneys, of course) to have a tasty snack. The evidence is the publication of exhaustive compendiums on the issue. So, it is far from settled. What's more, as image systems proliferate to encompass the billions of documents now maintained on paper and perhaps microform, legal cracks are bound to widen. The extent that a corporation's proposed image system will record documents with legal significance is the extent to which the legal environment should be understood. There is a trade-off, of course, when excessive legal concerns could outweigh the likely damages or the cost of insurance, but finding that point requires an understanding of the issue.

11.1 Optical image records as evidence

Thousands of court cases and regulatory hearings are resolved each year based on the quality of documentary evidence. Many of these documents are copies rather than originals, and therefore the subject has been addressed at some length in the Federal and Uniform Rules of Evidence and in greater detail by the Uniform Photographic Copies of Business and Public Records as Evidence Act (UPA). Further, three states (Louisiana, Missouri, and Virginia) have modified their statutes to cover electronic images specifically. Still, court cases have been decided on statutes, codes, and cases developed with respect to microforms. The criteria are:

- **Best-evidence criterion.** Courts require that written evidence is the best available documentation. In general, therefore, a photocopy, microform, or electronic image is not acceptable if the original is known to exist. In at least one case, an insurance company kept originals, despite its image system. Then, it tried to use these electronic records as evidence because it could not locate the originals. The plaintiff won by proving that the originals still existed; therefore, the copy was not acceptable. Incidentally, the fictional case in the film *Verdict* suggests that this rule of evidence can be safely ignored. Not true.

- **Normal-course-of-business criterion.** Even when the facsimile copy is the best available evidence, in most cases, it must have been recorded in that form during the normal course of business. Thus, if it is the practice of a company to keep paper originals, but to occasionally substitute copies without compelling reasons, those copies would be at risk in court. However, if the exceptions were made under compelling circumstances, and those circumstances had been formalized in written procedures, then they would meet the normal-course-of-business criterion.

- **Statutory provisions.** If a statute requires original documentation, directly or indirectly (the latter by prohibiting copies), then all bets are off. Courts will bypass these statutory restrictions only under the most exceptional circumstances.

- **Permissibility versus admissibility.** Issues on evidence constitute de facto trials within de jure trials. Many factors determine whether a specific piece of evidence is admissible—statutes and codes are almost always subject to interpretation.

So far so good. The theory continues: electronic images are a minor variation of microforms; therefore, no new obstacles stand in the way of using them as evidence. Unfortunately, one little problem intrudes. Electronic images are derived from bitstreams and those bitstreams have undergone several manipulations and are subject to subsequent improper manipulations. That middleman activity weakens their status as a sustainable equivalent of an original document. Some witnesses have been reluctant to confirm an image hardcopy as something they wrote (see FIG. 11-1). Given the factors described in the next section, this arcane technical issue can be exploited by defense attorneys.

11.2 Factors and significance

At least 12 factors affect the standing of documents as evidence. Some vary in different cases and others exert a steadier influence. Whatever the situation,

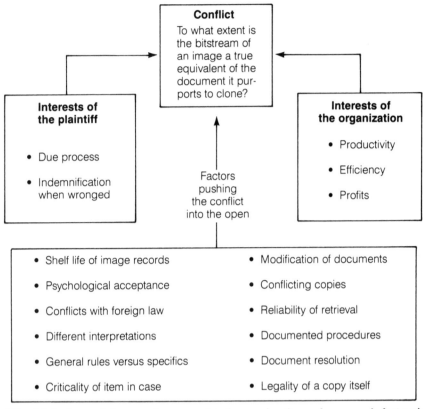

Fig. 11-1. Imaged documents are a step from microforms because of electronic manipulation. Unfortunately, imaged documents are more vulnerable in court than microforms.

the effects are all negative from the standpoint of image processing. Each one can be used to challenge image documents submitted by the opposing party.

- **Shelf life of image records.** If the reliability period of the storage medium that holds the document can be shown to be less than the age of the document itself, it can be challenged in court. Even when it is more, the defendant might have to prove that all humidity and temperature conditions were controlled during the entire time of storage. Manufacturers warrant shelf life for 10 or more years, but only under prescribed environmental conditions.

- **Psychological acceptance.** As mentioned previously, if a witness is reluctant to identify an image document as the one he or she wrote or prepared on paper, it will not likely be accepted as evidence. In a few cases, a judge might intervene by lecturing on the fine points of image records. However, the damage, from the viewpoint of the jury at least, has been done. Subsequent instructions to the jury to ignore an earlier opinion of the witness might not be effective.

- **International standards.** Most foreign courts have been slower to accept electronic facsimile records as evidence. This is of great significance for multinational companies and those engaged in international trade. In the United States, practices not in contravention of law are considered legal until proven otherwise. In other countries, the opposite is true. Even in Great Britain, which provided the foundation of American law, the courts are reluctant to jump from microfilm to image facsimiles.

- **Hearings versus courts.** Not all legal proceedings occur in courtrooms. Some hearings occur before regulatory boards, which often use different rules of evidence, even though the financial consequences can be the same as a court case. Moreover, different regulatory boards might differ in their interpretation of codes that they agree upon in principle. This factor is of particular interest to government contractors.

- **System versus media.** The goal of having courts accept optical disk records is oversimplified. A CD-ROM is likely to have greater standing than a WORM disk, and a WORM disk is likely to have greater standing than a rewritable disk. The reason is that each level in the hierarchy affords greater opportunity for data manipulation and thus degrades the potential reliability. Further, within one type, different technologies can rate different standings. One version could have a longer shelf life than another or be more prone to accidental modification—especially if the record is older.

- **Criticality of the document in question.** Few cases hinge on a single document. Rather, many (perhaps thousands of) documents typically are submitted in a single case. Challenges to some might not be as significant as to others. Or the evidence might be immaterial. The more critical the document, the more opposing attorneys will tend to question its reliability. It follows that experience with getting less important documents accepted could provide a false sense of security.

- **Bona fide modifications to the record.** Any modification to a document (as opposed to an update to a separate index file) could risk it in court. These modifications include the removal of noise, the use of optical character recognition (for all but printed bar codes and true OCR characters), and annotations (other than those recorded on separate overlay records). Exceptions can be made for normal-course-of-business annotations, but the burden of proof would be on the defendant.

- **Individually-retained copies.** If the plaintiff has retained a copy of the document in question, that copy is more reliable than the image records, and a conflict exists between the two, it does not take genius to figure the outcome. On the other hand, the plaintiff can question the reliability of the defendant's copy.

- **Practical reliability of retrieval.** If the defendant can prove that data decay (section 10.2) has set in and that the plaintiff no longer has absolute assurance of being able to retrieve all of the related documents from a logical set, the plaintiff's case will be weakened. Fortunately, this factor is moot for the time being. For all practical purposes, the oldest image records as of 1991 are no more than seven years old, and the vast majority are less than three years old.

- **Documentation on procedures and operations.** When a corporation relies on the normal-course-of-business criterion, it had better be able to document the applicable procedures and attest to their reliability—even if they must clearly demonstrate that the document at issue was processed under those procedures.

- **Document resolution.** The theory is that the record, whether on microform or an electronic medium, should have the same resolution as the original. That works fine for wirephotos, dot matrix printouts, and other matter that has already been prepared in a pixel format, but most documents are continuous. There are no pixels. The ink starts at one point and ends at another. So, the resolution issue turns to the degree to which the eye can consciously distinguish features and items on the document. Have you hugged your ophthalmologist recently?

- **Illegal copies.** Federal law prohibits copying many types of documents (with explicit exceptions). Therefore, any electronic facsimile copy of one of these documents could be challenged in court. The documents include any copyrighted material (unless permission has been obtained from the copyright holder), U.S. government securities, currency, bank notes, postage stamps, money orders (and similar documents issued by foreign governments), certificates of citizenship, draft registration cards, passports, and military and other federal identification badges and cards. It's a safe bet that more than a few image systems violate these restrictions daily, especially postage stamps on envelopes.

The point is again made that although these factors strain the feasibility of image processors, they can and will be exploited by either party in a case when it is to their advantage to do so. On the other hand, some offsetting trends could eventually bypass this legal obstacle course. Each case will nudge courts toward acceptability, rather than rejection in borderline cases.

The first of these trends is the internal use of electronic imaging by the courts themselves. In some cases, this extends to documents that have legal standing in their own right. Also, the use of image records has increased at a pace much faster than occurred with microforms—especially among government agencies. The latter will also encourage legislatures to act faster.

Given the technical issue of the bitstream and of the previous factors, offset by the expanding use of image records, the outlook is probably as favorable as vendors suggest (only if the subissues are properly addressed in specific cases). Moreover, the UPA code will probably be revised to cover image records, perhaps with periodic updates to take emerging technology into account. For example, once optical character recognition is perfected for handwritten forms (and records reduced to text files), then the records will not be as reliable as raster images. Still, the future is not now. Any organization that intends to install an image processing system or expand existing set-ups should carefully survey the legal consequences of relying on these facsimiles.

11.3 The copyright issue

The second major legal issue centers on copyright law and it is an issue that promises trouble:

- **Tailor-made singular text and reference books.** The costs of textbooks are beginning to reach prohibitive prices for many students with strained economic means. So, some publishers have made arrangements with professors and instructors to select material from existing books, print it (either on paper or on file), and pay only a proportional price. Authors would in turn receive a proportional royalty. So far, no one has challenged this practice in court because most textbook publishers insist on holding the copyrights. However, if it is done with books that have been copyrighted by the author and the contract does not allow for it, there could be some problems.

- **Eclectic text and reference books.** When eclectic selections of material are compiled into tailor-made imaged books, the problems become far more serious, unless explicit permissions were obtained from each copyright holder and any fees were paid. The poorly defined exception in copyright law that permits single copies to be made for educational purposes will not hold up if this practice grows.

- **Multiple image access to singular images.** If images are as good as paper, then concurrent access to copyrighted materials could be considered a law violation, aggravated if the users proceed to make hardcopies of selected pages. These laws are of considerable significance to libraries and publishers of scholarly journals and monographs who see image processing as an escape from their economic troubles.

• **Unregistered copyrights.** Almost everything written by anyone earns copyright protection the instant pen is set to paper (or data is sent to a file). Entering these documents into an image system might not be considered improper if the original is destroyed, for the same reason that the so-called time shifting of televised programs using videotape is not considered a violation of copyright law. However, it doesn't strain the imagination to see how imaging systems could be used to abuse the practice and distribute additional copies of copyrighted materials.

• **Liability of government instrumentalities.** Compounding the previous problems is the recent passage of federal legislation that specifies state institutions and their employees are liable for damages and other remedies for copyright infringement.

Part IV

Management

The management of the planning, implementation, and operation of an image processing system does not differ markedly from data processing in principal, but it does in degree. The culprit is the labor-intensive database orientation of the system, which begins with the planning phase. For many employees, it will be a new way of doing business. For management, it offers opportunities to

Fig. IV-1. A supervisor working with a staff employee. (Courtesy Automobile Club of Southern California)

further improve efficiency. However, these systems also require more attention to supervisory tasks and training for employees.

Figure IV-1, taken at the insurance processing division of the Automobile Club of Southern California, was posed, but it understates the reputation of that company. The average tenure of clerical employees is more than 15 years. Only top-notch supervisors and first-rate personnel policies can achieve a record of that caliber, especially in a metropolitan area. As a result, the installation of their image system worked very well. Not to say that it was without problems and glitches, but in every case, both the company and the vendor (IBM) rose to the challenge.

12

Planning

Set thine house in order

Isaiah 38.1

In some ways, this chapter is a summation of the salient points in the first eleven chapters, but the perspective changes from an emphasis on procedures to one of management concerns. Of these concerns, planning is perhaps the most important. It is a time when major mistakes can be avoided without paying the high cost of misdirected experience.

Of all the mistakes to be avoided, the most serious is to ignore the input of the employees and staff who operate the current manual systems (FIG. 12-1). An image system primarily automates existing procedures, and in most cases those procedures work fairly well. However, the inherent problems of paper files make this older option increasingly untenable.

The next three sections review macro analysis, cost analysis, and risk analysis, respectively. The discussion then turns to prototype options and concludes with an overview on the subject of trade-offs. *Trade-offs* are part of most decisionmaking, but do not confuse compromise with balance. Image systems are simply not easily compromised in some aspects. Buying too little image equipment, with respect to the needs of an organization, could cause new problems and a negative return on investment. For most organizations, image processing is a first rank investment and it could cause major reorganization.

12.1 Top down versus bottom up

In data processing, two common approaches to developing system programming are from top down and bottom up. Planning should encompass all of the requirements before the programming begins. Or so goes the theory. What happens in practice is that the planning is slipshod. As a result, the programming structure undergoes one or more major overhauls between the laying of the keel and the launching. The yacht all too often turns into a barge.

Fig. 12-1. The photograph suggests that lower level personnel and their work prevails long after upper levels have become history. As with image processing, the existing workforce best knows what needs to be done.

The problem looms no less for image systems, only the details are more widespread and more intense. The saving grace is that most systems have much in common; therefore, vendors can bring their knowledge to bear on new installations. Still, as mentioned in previous chapters, the greatest problem with imaging at the present time is the lack of expertise relative to the exploding demand.

How does one acquire instant expertise? First, gain an idea of what imaging can do and what it cannot do (or what it can do only at prohibitive expense). This doesn't require much: visit a few sites and read four or five good references on the subject. That will not produce expertise in the technical sense of the word, but it will provide enough of a perspective to proceed with the next step. Interestingly, the Association for Information and Image Management has just created a new division for education. So much for the top-down approach.

Turning next to the bottom-up perspective, the practical expertise comes from mapping out and understanding the internal operations of the organization. Some major consulting firms privately admit that 85 percent of the information they require for an assignment resides in the bowels of the customer's organization (although it takes a certain skill and objectivity to ferret it out). But image processing is not intended for solving problems. If major problems exist beyond those inherent in paper files, they must be resolved before imaging is considered; otherwise, the technology will only automate inefficiency.

In the process of mapping a healthy records management system, two characteristics will surface. First, it will become obvious to meet requirements with practical logic. Second, it will become apparent that physical documents are cumbersome. You must judge if an image system is the solution.

12.2 Macro analysis

As outlined in chapter 3, macro analysis consists of getting a firm grip on the numbers and lengths of records to be imaged; the logical indexing and linkage of those records (among themselves and with other databases); the workflow, access, and distribution requirements (including priorities); and modification and/or additions to material already on file. It is seldom necessary to consider hardware or proprietary software at this point. The technology already exists to meet almost any requirement; however, this is no guarantee that it will be affordable or will support the desired return on investment. Moreover, the need for outside consultants at this stage is also questionable—at least until some of the "spade work" has been done:

- **The database.** How many records are presently stored, and for how long in the active and inactive statuses? How long are they kept in an initial processing status? What kind of images are they (bilevel text, bilevel halftone, graytone, color)? How much storage will the total require? Will existing files be converted? If so, how far back?

- **The index and reference tables.** By what logic are records filed and retrieved? Are they grouped in folders? Will the existing logic hold for an image system, especially in light of any intended integrations with other databases, not presently worked with a manual equivalent? How much attribute information is imperative? Useful? Nice to have?

- **Processing.** What work is done with the records, and how often? Can it be streamlined? Can sequential processes be changed to concurrent, that is, is the sequential processing imposed by the single-copy availability milieu? What documents will be generated, and must they also be stored on the system? How will all this work be managed and controlled, i.e., how much by automation and how much by manual operators?

- **Communications.** Who needs to communicate with whom and how many images must be transmitted how often, how far, and to how many places (not counting local-area networks)? If the project will be installed at multiple sites, would it be more efficient to physically distribute the databases or to centralize them, or some of each? Compare efficiency in terms of cost, convenience, and logical indexing maintenance. The terms will seldom agree, so trade-offs are in the offering.

- **Special problems and critical points.** Are there any special problems with manual current systems? If so, and if they can be corrected, are they kept in an initial processing status?

If accurate numbers are used in the macro analysis, including planned expansions, then an equally accurate picture of the return on investment can be calculated (see FIG. 12-2). Minor inaccuracies in the data are random and tend to cancel one another out. Bear in mind the driving cost factors: the number and bitstream length of records stored in active status, the number of workstations, and the density of wide-area communications if needed.

12.3 Cost analysis

The fundamentals of cost analysis are covered in Business 101, and those principles underwrite the elementary spreadsheet model for image systems outlined in Appendix D. This section discusses the type and nature of most of the cost elements and operating factors. They are similar, but not identical to those that surround most data processing systems. Except for the early transaction-based systems, data processing tends to reduce the number of necessary personnel and free space. As for capital versus operating costs, the differences, save for depreciation, can be overlooked on the first cut.

- **Planning costs.** Planning costs can vary from negligible to millions of dollars. Planning can be done in-house on an other-duties-as-assigned basis or by a major consulting contract. Whether these costs should be linked to the project is an organizational decision, but if that decision is postponed until the planning is complete, the answer is no. The investment would have become a sunk cost.

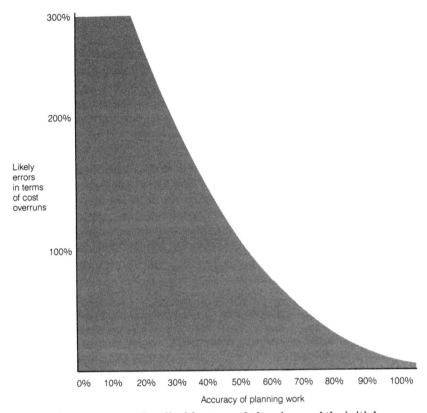

Fig. 12-2. Few systems work well without sound planning, and the initial or macro planning is the most important. This power curve illustrates the effect of how a few key parameters set the optimum size and configuration of a system.

- **Hardware and network equipment.** Of all items, the hardware and network equipment can be most accurately estimated, or so goes the theory. Unfortunately, specific capabilities and vendor prices vary widely for roughly the same capabilities (though as competition heats up and products and systems become more standardized, the prices become more similar). One approach is to use a range of prices and compute worst-case and best-case projections. The other is to select a tentative vendor and try to wheedle lower cost parameters out of him.

- **Software.** Depending on the complexity of the system, software can cost from 10 to over 100 percent more than the hardware. The costs can be divided into three subcategories: use of the vendor's software package, modifications and templating of that package, and original programming. Notice that as the vendors gain experience, more and more custom requirements will be built into productivity software; therefore, the cost will be driven down. This progress accumulates monthly and could suddenly jockey an "also-ran" vendor into first place in the economic race.

- **Supervisory personnel.** A system will probably increase the number or at least the skill levels of the supervisors. Managing a major automated system is more complex than managing stacked-shelves of paper. The supervisor-to-worker ratio is a function of the intensity of the processing.

- **Clerical personnel.** In most systems, the number of clerical personnel will be reduced, usually to a greater dollar extent than the increase in pay rates (if any) for those remaining. Accurate calculations here depend on accurate calculations of two of the driving factors that are summarized at the end of the previous section: storage parameters and number of workstations (factored for unusual processing requirements).

- **Space.** Almost without exception, image processing frees space, but the cost accounting of that space is problematic. Can it be sold, or sublet, or can its lease be broken? Can it be used for other purposes? Alternatively, can other functions be transferred to it and the former space be gotten rid of? If the space remains, will its vacuum suck in new functions that the company doesn't really need?

- **Training.** The cost of training, beyond that provided in the installation agreement, can range from negligible to extensive. If it occurs mostly on the job, it would be part of the supervisor expenses, except for training areas that do not contribute to operations. Sometimes a year or more is required to bring clerical operators up to full proficiency with all forms of acquisition and processing. However, they can be fully productive with a limited selection after a month or two.

- **Other operating expenses.** One option is to use a formula based on the number of employees and/or workstations and workloads. In other cases, they can be itemized. Not the least of these expenses is the cost of optical disks. A terabyte of stored information costs in the neighborhood of $100,000, and WORM disks, which are popular, cannot be reused. Interestingly, a few organizations find it more economical to rely on magnetic storage at the front end and optical tape afterwards. If this is the case, the entire cost picture will change markedly.

- **Taxes, depreciation, and lost opportunity costs.** Each organization has its own guidelines for cost accounting. Lost opportunity costs, however, are often ignored. These losses are sizable in large systems that are installed over a period of three or more years.

- **Factors and assumptions.** Factors and assumptions address cost overruns, inflation, growth, gain of market share, etc. A best-case/worst-case approach, using a what-if program, is the only hope here. Be leery if only the best-case assumptions generate a positive ROI.

12.4 Risk analysis

Risk implies failure, but the definition of failure varies. It can mean a total collapse at one extreme or 90 percent of the projected cost savings at the other. Fortunately, few failures in image processing exist to date and the same could be said for early data-processing installations. They concentrated on "bread-and-butter" heavy-duty transaction systems—especially those with enough economic incentive to compel automation. Similarly, the first wave of image systems concentrated on meeting compelling needs, most of which also resulted in marked cost savings.

Yet, as data processing grew beyond this realm into management information and decision support systems, the failure rate increased. Wishful thinking would presume that image processing will avoid this pitfall. Certainly, many of the existing systems have not quite lived up to their full billing. Therefore, decisionmakers should at least consider the various sources of failure and assure themselves that no one of them would likely do the project in. Alternatively, a combination of problems would defeat the effectiveness of the intended system. Arguably, the five most-common sources of failure or shortfall are:

- **Marketing or strategic failures.** This item is tough to measure, but the potential strategic advantage of an image system is often the deciding factor to install one, irrespective of up-front costs. That is, if the company pinned its hopes on a system for a strategic advantage that never materialized, the system is a failure even if it did reduce costs or increase productivity. These benefits would only be a consolation prize. On the other hand, if the market share or other strategic goal is reached, it could be difficult to attribute it to the image system. Incorrectly attributing strategic gains to a system, especially at a small first phase, and then going ahead with a major installation could be disastrous.

- **Shortcomings in reaction time.** Image systems are supposed to vastly improve retrieval times, and in practice almost all of them live up to the billing. But sometimes planners develop excessively stringent realtime standards that can be met only by a major cost increase. When this is discovered, the choice is therefore to pay the much higher express freight or accept service on the local.

- **Inadequate software and control.** This is the most common type of failure, as indeed it is in data processing. It can stem from poor planning or analysis, from buying an inadequate vendor software package, or from incompetent programming. Whatever the reason, it can usually be corrected . . . for a price. That price, in extreme cases, could mean scrapping the entire system or at least changing to another vendor for subsequent phases (this has already happened in at least one case). However, software failure at the database management level is rare; the vendors have come close to perfecting it. By contrast, applications programming runs headlong into the same well-known obstacles that beset data-processing software. The offsetting advantage is that the documents themselves provide a sort of logical anchor.

- **Hardware or communications failure.** Hardware and communications failures are rare, except in an occasional downtime during critical periods or peak loading above design levels. A bitstream is a bitstream. Shortcomings in the form of delayed transmissions are types of reaction time failures. But incompatibilities among different systems intended for integration could be a problem. These incompatibilities can include records stored in a nonstandard format. Everything can be fixed, of course, but at what point does the "fix" degenerate into technological slop?

- **Failures stemming from delayed implementation.** This very subjective aspect of risk analysis derives from advances in technology and lowered prices after the agreement is drafted and perhaps signed, but before it has been implemented. Opportunities for gaining a strategic edge (when that opportunity is bona fide) can evaporate, or competitors might take advantage of the new technology and lower cost to get to the marketplace first, so to speak. Perhaps this risk is greater for vendors than customers, but it is bound to affect at least some of the latter.

12.5 Prototype options

A *prototype* is a model of a planned product, service, or procedure. The idea is almost always to test unknowns before a commitment is made to proceed with full-scale production. Accordingly, prototype results could suggest to go ahead, majorly modify, scale down, completely abandon the project, or in a few rare cases, to go further than originally planned. See section 13.2 for the difference between a prototype and a pilot project.

- **Macro installation.** This model uses a full-scale setup, usually one found in another operation, to test a new application, albeit not necessarily with the full volume of traffic. Some vendors, notably Wang Laboratories, offer to install a test system on a trial basis for 90 days or so. However, if custom software is required, this option is not very useful.

- **Micro installation.** This model uses low-cost desktop image processing systems to test certain aspects of a project on a small scale. Several
  of these desktops can be linked by a common local-area network. The
  utility, however, is limited to the micro aspects of image systems. It just
  doesn't have the heft to support a full perspective.

- **Computer models.** This data-processing computer simulation of a
  proposed system is especially useful when complex programming is
  required. Sample images can be recorded on magnetic storage, and
  entered by way of a FAX machine, if necessary.

- **Manual walkthroughs.** This option simply uses supervisory and
  technical labor to simulate the electronic system—similar to a
  walkthrough of conventional programming. It can be as simple or as
  complex as appropriate.

No prototypes are intended for orientation and general education. Site visits and reading are the means for that. Rather, a prototype should focus on
obtaining information on unknown factors or uncalculated magnitudes that are
necessary before a firm installation agreement should be signed.

12.6 Trade-off considerations

Decisionmaking on long-term commitments and projects almost always
involves trade-offs. The so-called deluxe approach is rarely affordable, and the
bare-bones option often begs failure from the onset. Where then, are the soft
spots of compromise?

For image systems, most of these soft spots are at the high end. A certain
threshold set-up mass is required to achieve goals and eliminate former manual
practices. Until that level is reached, dual systems will be worse than manual
alone. It will increase costs and introduce conflicts—especially if different
indexing algorithms are used. This situation is somewhat similar to building
an automobile. Leave out the chassis, the engine, the drive train, the steering
column, or just about anything else of significance, and it will lose it's utility.
Even omitting the heater or the air conditioner will make it uncomfortable to
use in many environments. So what is left to haggle over are the deluxe acces-
sories and options.

One of the best ways to get a handle on this is to participate in a vendor's
customer advisory group (if he will allow it prior to signing an agreement).
These groups meet regularly and provide benefits and insights to both parties.
Wang Laboratories calls their group the *Strategic Accounts Council* (combined
with its Executive Contact Program of one-on-one working relationships
between their executives and customers). IBM calls their group the *Customer
Advisor Council*. In practice, most of the discussions focus on the very fine

points of image systems. However, the severity of problems that arise from any degree of corner cutting osmose throughout the discussions.

Thus, the best approach on trade-off analysis is to start with the level and scope of a system that will meet all nonnegotiable requirements with essentially no risk of failure. From that baseline, the marginal cost and likely return on investment for increases to quantity or quality can be gauged.

Should each operator have his or her own workstation, or can some parts be shared? Can some records be shifted to inactive status earlier and thus cut down on the on-line storage hardware? The list goes on and on, and probably a mini trade-off exists for how many are considered. More subjective trade-offs address paying a higher price to a vendor who has a strong reputation for reliability or buying excess capability to accommodate possible future expansions. Again, the list goes on and on.

13

Implementation

The process of the law is vexatious,
its magnificence is in its execution.

Legal maxim

The implementation of an image system can be a traumatic experience for a large corporation and its employees. The simplicity of the image database concept hides the actual technical complexity of the equipment and the resulting changes to processing that must occur. Probably, no single problem will be particularly difficult, but the collective effect of these irritants can be aggravating.

The primary responsibility for the installation is one of the most important factors to consider. At least four options exist and three of them work well under most circumstances. Bear in mind that installation is not the same as ongoing management, unless the agreement expressly calls it. The organization should wean itself from the vendor as soon as possible, except for maintenance and service agreement work. At the present, the relationships between some vendors and their respective customers can almost be described as fraternal. The technology is so fascinating and the benefits are so obvious that cooperation is exceptional. But then, so are some relationships between parents and their children. If it is exceptional, the relationship should change with time.

Other sections in this chapter cover phasing, agreements, and some lessons learned. With respect to the last item, more than a thousand have been documented by various vendors. So, only a sample can be described here—the ones that seem to crop up most often in discussions.

13.1 Project management options

Four options for pursuing an image system are available (FIG. 13-1). The project could be placed under the operational control of a vendor until it is implemented. Or it could be placed under the control of an independent consultant, usually one that is primarily involved with image systems. Or the corporation can serve as its own project manager.

125

	Advantages	**Disadvantages**
Vendor	• Usually a master of his own technology • A good trade-off between cost and value	• Comparatively limited selection of hardware • Might lack sensitivity to customer's needs
Value-added consultant	• Widest choice of hardware and software • Best source of wide expertise	• Highest up-front costs • Complex layers of responsibilities during installation
Independent consultant	• Single mind dedicated to a single project • Objectivity	• Rarely in a position to control vendors • Might not know when to back off
Internal management	• Generally the lowest cost • Maximum control over installation	• Lack of expertise could be a disaster • Warranties much more limited

Fig. 13-1. A corporation can elect to use a vendor or a consulting firm to oversee the planning and implementation of an image system, or it can choose to go it alone. If the latter, at least one executive really needs to know about image systems.

The vendor option is really two options. The first is based on a primary vendor, such as IBM, FileNet, DEC, Wang, or Kodak. The second is a value-added vendor, who subcontracts with specific vendors to put together a system that meets a client's requirements.

Surveys indicate that most companies prefer to serve as their own project managers. However, until expertise in image processing becomes more widespread, the vendor options will continue to dominate—at least for larger installations. In one compromised approach, a vendor is used for the initial phase until it proves operational. Then, internal management is used for subsequent phases:

• **Vendor option.** The vendor option is the most common for new installations. The primary vendors either sell entire packages or work in close partnerships with other vendors to the point that complete packages that work like systems are available. The real problem with this option, however, is more subtle. If existing computers and networks are relied upon as much as possible, the choice of vendors and perhaps the image requirements options will be severely restricted.

- **Value-added consultant option.** This variation on the vendor option is particularly useful when no vendor can support all requirements efficiently (which often occurs with very large systems). The problem is that very few individuals are masters of the entire landscape of technology offered by hundreds of vendors. That is, some value-added consultants tend to specialize in relatively few combinations. Therefore, it might be necessary to compare the technical aspects of competing bids for other than lowest cost. The road to hell has been resurfaced a dozen times with low-cost bids.

- **Independent consultant option.** This option is rare and tends to work well only for very small functional-level setups. However, some consultants are worth their fees when they complete a macro analysis and draw a list of specifications and requirements. The great advantage is objectivity—especially if the work is done without specific vendors in mind. Some consultants are also very good at organizing training.

- **Internal management option.** This option is preferred by most companies and most would probably choose it if they had the necessary expertise. Even if this option was chosen, the vendors will still exert a more influential role than with comparative data processing projects. For the most part, the vendor's enthusiasm for their products is contagious. The customers can become mesmerized.

13.2 Phasing

Phasing is also an important element of implementation. Making a major mistake can be more disastrous than choosing the wrong management option; minor mistakes have a way of getting washed out.

Individual workstations are not difficult to install, but a poor sequence of activities can wreak havoc on corporate performance. Phasing also depends on the project level: function, department, or enterprise. Function-level installations rarely have more than one phase, but enterprise-level ones can have ten or more. The department-level installations present a somewhat different situation. The phases will more than likely need close coordination; neither too much nor too little should be bitten off at first.

Figure 13-2 pictures four common phasing approaches. Bear in mind the differences between prototypes, pilots, and production phases. A prototype (as discussed in section 12.5) is an experiment, not an installation. By contrast, a pilot is intended to be the first phase or at least the core of the first phase of a production. If the first phase composed 40 workstations, the pilot might have only enough hardware to support three to five workstations. However, what is installed should become an integral part of the entire phase. That is not the case with prototypes.

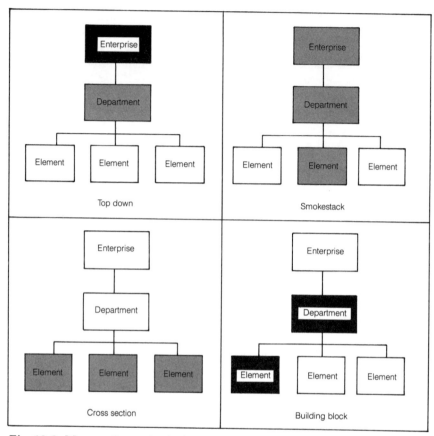

Fig. 13-2. Many options exist for implementing a system, but most are variations on one of four approaches. Moreover, the database intensity of imaging favors the building block approach, though the other options can be overlapped with some form of prototype.

- **Top down approach.** This software-type approach installs the complete database management software (minus application inserts) from the top level of the intended system down through every departmental or functional level. Afterwards, the specific applications are added. Unfortunately, although it sounds wonderful, it rarely works. The logic for running all of the elements already exists and needs to be automated efficiently—either as is or in a more streamlined way.

- **Smokestack approach.** This approach simultaneously installs pilots for different levels in an enterprise-level system. It is sometimes called *vertical development*. It differs from the top-down approach in that representative sections at all levels become functional at the same time. This approach is useful when enterprise-wide integration is the key consideration, but that is uncommon.

- **Cross section approach.** This approach starts with pilots in different functional areas of a departmental-level system, or in different departments of an enterprise-level system. As an alternative, one unit can be made fully operational before the pilots are installed in the sister elements. This approach is especially useful when the integration of interdepartmental processing is the prevailing requirement.
- **Building block approach.** This approach is probably the most common. One complete unit is installed before any other units. It is a sound approach when integration is not a dominant consideration, and perhaps even when it is. This approach also lends itself to changing from being vendor-managed to being internally managed for subsequent phases. This is the approach to use unless a compelling reason exists to elect a different route.

13.3 The agreement

Sooner or later, an organization that intends to install an imaging system must come to terms with one or more vendors or a value-added vendor. This agreement could be based on lowest bid, on established reputation, or on any other criterion, but certain elements are common to all:

- **Responsibilities.** Who is responsible for what, and at what point do these responsibilities change? Every point of responsibility that is left ambiguous begs for complications down the road. The better vendors will insist on these provisions even more than customers. Benjamin Franklin said that experience runs an expensive school, but fools will learn in no other, and scarcely in that one. It is surprising how many companies fail to recognize that their proposed agreements could be an application to attend that well-known school (and pay the high tuition).
- **Scope of work.** Exactly what will the vendor or vendors provide and when? What are goods and what are services? If any two places in the agreement require as much detail as can be packed in, this is one of them. Without this detail, the agreement is purely a pig in a poke. Moreover, it is to the vendor's benefit to label everything a service; to the customer, a good. The latter affords a better standing in court if a breach of contract occurs and it also supports definition-of-performance standards.
- **Performance standards.** The plan should ensure that maximum peak loads and damage limitations are included for when overloads occur. Given the complexities and options for most elements of an image system, this section of the agreement can easily run to 50 pages. In practice, performance standards for specific pieces of equipment are available from the vendors and are attached, or at least referenced, in agreements.

- **Price or cost basis.** This topic needs little discussion, but if too many unknowns exist, the plans become little more than wishful thinking.

- **Training.** Don't overlook training. The vendor has the expertise, not the customer. How much, how often, and how many measurable results need to be nailed firmly in the agreement.

- **Warranties.** Warranties put teeth into the goods and services specifications, and for performance standards. Warranties are especially important if the vendor is also the project manager for installation. Specific product warranties do not cover the whole system operation unless the vendor makes a point of it in the agreement.

- **Service and maintenance.** These points could be covered by the warranty provisions, but they are often separate—especially if the vendor offers an optional service contract. Make sure the cutoff date for service during installation and the warranty period is clearly distinguished from ongoing maintenance. Service contracts tend to be more expensive than ad hoc service. However, if reducing downtime to an absolute minimum is essential, the higher cost could be offset by the effects of increased productivity.

- **Documentation.** The vendor should supply full documentation for the operation of all items installed. Insist on it. IBM inundates their customers with technical information. Other vendors might supply very little documentation.

- **Facilities.** This topic covers where the system is to be installed, power supplies and environmental prerequisites, and the work areas for the vendor and subcontractors. This provision is often glossed over—a mistake.

- **Interim progress evaluations and acceptance.** It is okay to stray on the side of formal progress reports and mutual evaluations, and of course formal criteria for acceptance, e.g. test results and how thorough those test are to be. It keeps everybody on their toes.

- **Built-in capabilities to accept expansions.** This point is optional, but if the plan is to expand beyond the scope of the agreement, the topics covered should be as stringent as humanly possible.

Perhaps the most important point is the sensitivity of the vendor(s) to corporate requirements. This sensitivity defies inclusion in agreements, but if any doubt exists before the agreement is signed, it's a safe bet the shortcoming will manifest itself in a continuous series of problems—just like many marriages.

13.4 Lessons learned

Despite the newness of image processing, an impressive list of "lessons learned" have surfaced and been documented. Moreover, as noted in the previous chapter, some vendors have created customer advisor committees to capitalize on these lessons for future installations, as well as to meet current needs. Some of these lessons apply to planning, some to installing, and some to systems managing, and a few to all. Still, it is during installation that these lessons coalesce.

- **Listen to clerical employees.** This is one lesson that all vendors agree on. As stated many times throughout this book, the clerical employees are the experts. They will seldom speak up if not asked. But when asked, they will not hesitate to present complete and detailed pictures and provide useful input when several automation options are being considered.

- **Deal with the complexities of unusual cases.** Any system that is designed to fully automate the most complex case imaginable will never work—not today, not tomorrow, not ever. Thus, preparing software for the most complex cases might double the programming load. For example, the insurance division of the Automobile Club of Southern California manually underwrites policies for Rolls-Royces and other motor cars of high repute; everything else goes through the ringer. The results, however, are stored in the same image system.

- **Don't discard documents prematurely.** Errors will occur during acquisition scanning and will need to be corrected. If the originals have been destroyed, it will be difficult and sometimes impossible to make the corrections. And during the early phases of installation, it might be necessary to run a dual system. At first, the automated system would be used for testing. Later, the older manual system would serve as a backup—until the company believes that it will work as intended.

- **Understand employee expectations.** Low-level employees are often the most conscientious. They become upset if the system reaction times are too slow, and often blame themselves for the delays—especially during installation and testing. In other words, it is the automation that should come up to manual standards, not the opposite.

- **Personnel practices.** Dozens of approaches have been tried: separated acquisition from processing versus combined tasks, rotated personnel assignments versus specialization, four 10-hour workdays per week versus the standard five 8-hour days, and scheduled breaks versus flexible breaks. At Pittsburgh National Bank, rotated assignments reduced boredom and error rates because each employee became aware of the problems caused by his or her own mistakes. Other companies have had the opposite experience. Many options exist for personnel management practices, and whether they work or not depends on many circumstances that are unique to each installation.

- **Training.** Never underestimate the amount of training required to bring employees up to full proficiency with image systems. A year or more is not uncommon. A great deal of expertise and patience is needed when dealing with the myriad of circumstances that arise when working with automated equipment.

- **OCR and bar codes.** So far, OCR and bar codes appear to be helpful when entering index and attribute data, but they do not work well in all systems. In the first place, not all documents lend themselves to this technique; therefore, some can use it and others cannot. Next, the common versus specific information relevant to each document is a problem. Finally, OCR works better than bar codes in so called "clean" environments, and bar codes work better in so-call "dirty" environments. The adjectives refer to the condition of the documents and/or the loss of quality control during acquisition, not to physical dirt. Stores and inventory systems are good examples of "dirty" environments. In fact, the options all have distinct advantages and disadvantages. And don't hold your breath waiting for OCR that can read and decipher handwriting.

- **Operating characteristics.** The weight of opinion so far is that employees prefer a straightforward means of using the system. They seldom need neat little icons on the screen or mouse devices (except in certain specialized applications). Any procedure that seems user unfriendly to a novice becomes ho-hum routine to dedicated employees within a month.

- **Executive use.** When executives and other personnel are expected to use the system on a casual basis, however, the access does need to be more user friendly—somewhat like the optional-use pull-down menus in popular software packages. Unfortunately, this is easier said than done, unless the vendor has built the optional access into his productivity software.

- **Mixing data processing and image processing workstations.** The lesson here is to think twice before mixing data processing and image processing workstations, except in the limited case of text data that must be processed in conjunction with image records. The two functions require different skill levels and it can introduce many priority conflicts.

- **Forms.** Many forms are shaded or screened. Some scanners overreact to this shading and obliterate the text. Make sure that the scanners purchased can filter this background "noise" or alternatively, that the forms can be redesigned.

- **Customers.** It is very easy to lose sight of the ultimate purpose of image systems and focus instead on the fascinating technology. What really counts is how well the customer is served in practice.

Fig. 13-3. Forget the neat workstations pictured in vendor brochures. These workstations are home, for the better part of the day, to operators. This workstation is only mildly personalized, some are miniature museums with hundreds of posted items.

Readers are encouraged to send suggestions for expanding or modifying entries in this section (or for any item in the book for that matter). As mentioned, the image-processing community has become something of a fraternity, and any criticism that is even the slightest bit constructive is sought after (FIG. 13-3).

14

Systems management

Happy are they that hear the detractions
and can put them to mending.

Shakespeare

Any system installation can be a traumatic experience, and some veterans describe it as the immoral equivalent of war. Arguably, this environment is inherent in the installation process, but it is unacceptable once the system becomes operational. Few organizations or individuals can tolerate constant disruptions and changes to the systems they depend on. This doesn't mean that supervision can take a back seat. The procedures to ensure efficient operation of the system, beyond the indispensable human touch that good managers evince continuously, should be more systematic and predictable—primarily based on compiled data (manual or automated—focused primarily on situations that warrant intervention).

On the other hand, image systems have led some companies to reorganize in order to take advantage of their features. The necessary experience to make wise changes might not accrue until after the system has been in operation for a year or so. Those changes in turn could suggest modifications to the system configuration, or at least a different set-up for subsequent phases.

Once again, an image system can permeate the entire flow of information in any organization—or at least all of the information that is reduced to writing. When this permeation occurs, the supervisory and management tasks will be much greater than "some subset of an information manager's job description" (FIG. 14-1).

14.1 Supervision and troubleshooting

The overarching question for image system managers is: to what extent are the supervisory tasks similar to manual systems, and to what extent are they different? Theoretically, the overlap exceeds 90 percent. Practically, it's a new ball game. The explanation is simple. First, an image system eliminates many chores, but the automation itself needs to be checked periodically. Second, an

Fig. 14-1. Supervisory tasks increase at an exponential rate that is relative to the number of workstations. Most of the increase arises from the speed with which image systems operate—somewhat similar to the breakdowns that occur when an intricate network becomes overloaded. (Courtesy FileNet)

image system will probably change procedures and reduce the number of employees, but it will upgrade the employees' skill levels. Third, the speed at which automation works will intensify the supervisory tasks that remain. Fourth, the automation will open windows of opportunity that are not presently attended to. Fifth, these points will work to change the balance of the tasks.

Accordingly, the subject of image system supervision warrants its own book. All that can be mentioned here is to comment briefly on how the bidding changes for generic task areas. The list was derived from a FileNet slide entitled "The Manual Effort in Paper Flow."

- **Logging documents in and out.** This task all but disappears in automated systems, except with transferring optical disks or other storage media (usually under the control of a few key individuals). Indexing and recording attribute information takes its place, and the tendency is to extract and record more information into these files than was the case with manual system indexes. However, some systems keep an automated book with every access to every document or folder.

- **Suspense file management.** The logic of this task does not change, but most of it is automated. For those systems that need suspense dates, one is assigned at the time of acquisition (usually with a priority code). From that point forward, the program tracks those dates. The better kinds automatically increase the priority code as the current date approaches the suspense deadline. Thus, supervisory tasks shift in emphasis to systemic management in lieu of the old focus on trouble-shooting specific cases. These exceptional cases still occur, but at a much lower frequency.

- **Sorting, routing, and prioritizing.** Here again, the logic does not change, but the bulk of the work is automated based on algorithms that match index and attribute codes to automated tables of instructions and information on workstations/operators. Thus, the supervisors can also focus on systemic problems, rather than repeatedly massaging the problem cases. The surprising thing about this shift in emphasis is that few vendors mention it in their literature.

- **Performance measurement and evaluation.** This task expands, but is almost always supported by programming that compiles statistics from index and access data. If anything, the process can be too detailed and abusive. For example, the morale problems that develop when, say, telephone operators are evaluated based on continuous computer monitoring.

- **Staff load balancing.** Of necessity, at least in large systems, this task is usually automated and manual intervention only occurs in complex situations. Most systems keep track of processing assignments put into queue for various operators and then route new cases to the stations that have the shortest-factored queue. A *factored queue* is the computation of the time required to complete the work. The supervisory tasks focus on upgrading employee skills, or if inherently limited, keeping the workload (and paygrade) at an appropriate level.

- **Control of elapsed time.** This task is closely associated with prioritization and suspense file management. In manual systems, however, the suspense file is often adjunct to the log, leaving it to supervisors to know whether the deadlines are being met. In an automated system, this task is typically integrated into its cousins, and therefore is seldom of much concern by itself.

- **Training of new staff.** This task, per person, intensifies by a factor of three or more upon changing from a manual to an automated system. The reason, as noted in previous chapters, is that more and higher level skills are concentrated in fewer job descriptions. Some of the training is formal, using fictional cases on either a separate or virtual machine. Past this step, most training is the on-the-job type—probably the most taxing of supervisory responsibilities. A fine balance between resolute standards and patience greatly pays off—both in productivity and morale.

• **Quality control.** The ever present need for quality control makes no exception here, but image systems radically change the laundry list of items to be checked. The most-important aspect of quality control is verification of acquisition on three counts: the quality of each document must meet minimum standards (which vary with the document), the pages or documents in a set must be captured and linked, and the indexing and attribute information must be correct. The second most-troublesome area is the correctness of interactive processing. This is a human skill, and, given the speed of image systems, is the most critical task for supervisors. When quality control fails here, the mechanical effectiveness of the system only accelerates customer dissatisfaction. In practice, therefore, many supervisors integrate their training and quality control objectives.

Initiative level • Decision support algorithms that focus and perhaps intervene on a system as an entity	The programming required for this level of support system is often too expensive for the benefits obtained. Too many factors and subtleties affect the efficiency of a system.
Intervention level • Uses optimization to redirect processing • That failing, signals a supervisor with a menu of options	Investment in this level of software usually pays off, providing it does not attempt to supplant human judgment. The idea is to automate the camera, not the photographer.
Reactive level • Flags cumulative data and/or processing that exceeds norms • Can invoke elementary corrective actions	The additional programming required to effect this level usually pays for itself ten times over. It automates routine "decisions" that would otherwise consume untold manhours.
Compilation level • Statistical summaries of acquisitions, accesses, etc., to any level of detail set by the user	This is simple to program and often comes as part of any system. It consists of little more than identification of various bitstreams and bumping the appropriate counters.

Fig. 14-2. The hierarchy of automated systems management progresses from simple compilations to system-wide intervention programming. The power curve for return on investment starts early but usually levels off and turns down before the highest level is reached.

14.2 Automated management tools

Most of the tasks from the previous section describe management information systems. Many vendors offer this programming as part of the systems package, and others provide gates into their software where users can insert their own programming. Figure 14-2 illustrates the theoretical hierarchy of the four levels of automated management tools. In practice, each higher level builds on the programming of lower levels. The lower levels should be structured with that purpose in mind (technical note C.5 on relational versus hierarchical database structures).

- **Compilation level.** This level, when overused, has turned many executives away from automated management information systems. It simply notes transactions and bumps various counters—logic that most third graders would find boring. Moreover, it typically churns out reams of data and then passively challenges the user to make sense of it. If only this level will be employed, it is imperative to provide summary data on a few pages, and perhaps indicate where the sums fall outside the range of norms. All other data should be written to files for access as needed; for example, to check into a particular problem area.

- **Reaction level.** Reaction programming works by continually scanning resident and operating data and comparing it to norms. The most common application of reaction programming occurs in networks for redirecting traffic when the primary paths are loaded (thus, integrating with the next level of programming, at least at an elementary level). Typical examples range from automatically upping a priority code as a suspense date nears, to redirecting critical traffic to other experienced operators when a scheduled individual is absent, to controlling concurrent processing (e.g. automated flagging and rerouting a case when work on a later step is completed before an earlier one). That is, concurrent processing vastly improves productivity, but it sometimes runs afoul of logical sequence. These occasional glitches are tolerable if the system can react to them on time.

- **Intervention level.** Although most reaction software has some elements of if-then-else algorithms, more sophisticated applications use decision-support system logic (which admittedly is a branch of if-then-else decision points). The difference is that minor variations are taken into account and if the situation warrants interaction, the preparatory analysis will have been done. Supervisors are then free to concentrate on immediate problems. A classic example of pushing this level to the limit would be a complete redistribution of workload to other departments or functions when a system shutdown occurs.

- **Initiative level.** Applications at this level apply decision support logic to the system as an entity (what might be called macro- or meta-intervention). The idea is to assess the pattern of interventions or even just the statistical compilations to suggest changes to the way the system is run. However, the expertise and time required to program at this level often outweighs the benefits.

Superintending all of these levels composes a problem that crops up in too many systems of any kind. This problem is the slew of disconnects that often arise between the automated and the manual elements. The system signals a supervisor to take corrective action, which he or she does. Then, the same system proceeds to do what it was programmed to do, perhaps in contravention to the action that the supervisor took. More likely, changes will be made by one supervisor without updating the reports given to another.

As luck would have it, just as this section was being written, an example of this happened to me in the form of a changed reservation (albeit from a data processing, rather than an image processing system). No harm was done in this case, but upon becoming aware of the conflict, the reservations clerk immediately checked the computer record and found that it differed (correctly so) with an older printed output from before the reservation was changed. If a management information system is supported by automation, then the designer must ensure that the right hand knows what the left disk is doing.

14.3 Disposal of inactive records

Manual record management systems compel most organizations to dispose of inactive documents as soon as they age past the point of any legal or business requirement to keep them. Image systems eliminate that motivation on two counts. First, optical disks use less than one percent of the storage area needed for paper records. Second (at least for WORM disks and tape), the media cannot be reused. Thus, the temptation is to keep the data permanently because "the expense is negligible" and "one never knows when the information will be needed."

So far, this problem has lain dormant. The vast majority of image systems are no more than three years old (as of early 1991), and only a few of these converted older records to disk storage. Still, the problem will grow soon enough and will crash head-on with the ACM Code of Professional Conduct Canon V Human Welfare. This canon states that only the minimum essential data should be put in automated form, that access should be limited, and that the information should be destroyed as soon as practical.

The argument to make an exception to this canon is that image records are not data in the normal sense of the word and therefore can neither be processed nor compiled. Unfortunately, this argument just doesn't wash. First, the index and attribute data would be processable immediately. Second, most abuses concentrate on reading specific data, rather than running programs against a mass of it. Third, OCR for handwriting will eventually become practical; thus, any image record will be converted to text and become processable data. Admittedly, this is a negative note on which to end a positive book, and yet it is a harbinger of things to come.

Image systems can, in theory, store everything that is written within a corporation and keep it accessible for 30 or more years. The automation of customer information will probably increase tenfold, if not twentyfold, over the next 10 to 20 years.

The halcyon days of image processing won't last much longer. Within the next five years, the laggards will be rushing to keep up with progress and the technology itself will leap at new challenges. In the process, many of the side effects that came with data processing will grow here. A large measure of good judgment, expertise, and attention to detail is needed to avoid the mistakes that befell conventional data processing.

Appendix A
Application models

Actually, Homer was not written by Homer,
but by another man with the same name.

Another schoolboy response on a quiz

Image processing systems can be subdivided into different generic models, and those models vary depending on the criterion. Some writers stress industries; others stress the system and processing mechanics. This appendix veers to the latter, the idea of which was derived from an excellent presentation in InfoImage Basics: *Document Imaging, the Picture of Information* (Unisys Corporation) and some graphs that I saw while visiting the Eastman Kodak Company.

The four models are: transaction, folder, reference, and document generation. In practice, many systems combine two or three of these "models," but with infrequent exception, each system tends to revolve around just one model. As such, a generic model can provide a starting point or perspective for macro analysis.

The *transaction model* focuses on processing specific requirements and is closest to conventional data processing. The image system part is primarily a means to reduce paper. The *folder model* is also transaction or at least update oriented, but the focus is on linking the models to a folder or file with synergistic importance. Hence, this model relies more on image processing than data processing. The *reference model* is essentially a self-contained record unit that depends heavily on imaging. Lastly, the *document-generation model* uses image processing as springboard for a wider range of activities that go beyond records management.

A.1 Transaction-oriented model

The transaction-oriented model focuses on specific transactions and the processing required (FIG. A-1). As such, it comes close to data processing operations and it is sometimes adjunct to existing systems—primarily to reduce the

143

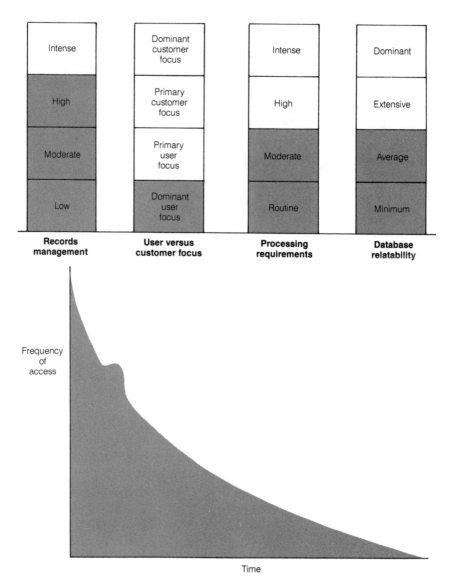

Fig. A-1. The transaction model concentrates the bulk of its processing at the front end and the subsequent processing is focused on ledger work. This model is often integrated with existing data processing systems.

paper documentation to electronic facsimile storage. Other installations, however, try a more fundamental realignment of processing so that the resulting system gives the appearance and advantages of having been designed as part of the original configuration. With little debate, banking and inventory operations favor this model. The bulk of the work is processing of specific actions, with the results posted to various ledgers, accounts, and other statistical compilations.

- **Records management.** Most transaction systems are records oriented—more for the audit trail than for processing after the entry ages a month or so. Subsequent processing tends to focus on the ledgers and other statistical roll-ups.

- **Customer versus user orientation.** The customer is secondary with respect to the system. Once that customer receives the order, is paid, or learns of the approval or disapproval of his application, the records become 99 percent user-oriented.

- **Processing.** Although transaction systems require extensive cumulative processing time, the programming tends to be routine—often well-documented and already in operation in other systems.

- **Relatability.** Virtually all transactions must be logged, but this relatability is limited to only a handful of compilations. However, the system will likely require maximum integration with existing data processors.

- **Access requirements versus time.** If the documents are acquisitioned before processing, then access times need to be short, if not instantaneous. If the acquisition steps occur after the initial processing, then minor delays in processing might be more tolerable.

- **Opportunities.** The potential is low if the data is already recorded in a data processing system. However, when that is not the case, the opportunities are the same as for any decision support system.

A.2 Folder-oriented model

The folder-oriented model is based on files or folders that represent individuals, functions, specific materials, and so forth (FIG. A-2). It varies from the transaction model in that access tends to be to the folder first, rather than an after the fact posted transaction. A personnel file system is a good example. An inventory control system tends to hover on the dividing line between this and the transaction model (as would a customer account system that is as oriented to customers as to ledgers). An insurance policy system could be either, depending how closely the processing claims are linked to policyholder folders.

- **Records management.** Probably the same as in transaction-based systems. The change in direction from action-to-folder to folder-to-action has little impact on the total workload. However, update actions tend to have more pages than routine transactions.

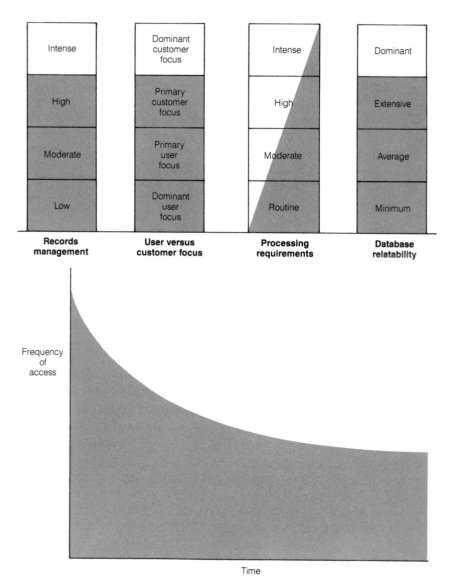

Fig. A-2. In the folder model, the collection of documents and transactions is strongly linked to files that represent individuals or easily identified entities. This model tends to be more customer oriented.

- **Customer versus user orientation.** In most cases, the intent of the system is to serve individuals or functions external to the system. This system is often used in conjunction with telephone calls from clients.

- **Processing.** Processing can range from occasional to intense in quantity, and the updates can also range from simple to complex. For example, changing an address is much easier than underwriting a request for an insurance policy for a custom built house in an earthquake zone.

- **Relatability.** Relatability requirements are usually limited to the current folder and to various reference tables. However, statistical roll-ups for management and strategic planning purposes require strong relatability and considerable attribute information that is recorded in index or supplementary data files.

- **Access requirements versus time.** Access to a folder is high during the first few days of its existence, and thereafter is ad hoc. But collective access to the folders in the system is level, as long as they remain in active status.

- **Opportunities.** These opportunities are similar to those that exist for transaction systems. Collective data analysis can be used for strategic planning and decision purposes, provided that the system and its indexes were configured with that objective in mind.

A.3 Reference-oriented model

The reference-oriented model breaks away from the common folder-and/or-transaction orientation and tends to place every item on an equal basis—even though each one might consist of a large collection of related documents (FIG. A-3). A library is the quintessential example, but the model goes far beyond the automated indexes found in many of them. It entails putting all or most references into image storage and eliminating the paper. The federal government probably won't store the Declaration of Independence and the Constitution, but many of the references stored in the Library of Congress are fair game—especially if the exploding registered copyrighted publication era continues. Libraries aren't the only application for image storage; in practice, engineering firms have been the heaviest users of this model so far.

- **Records management.** The emphasis on records management is the index. Once logged into the system, the index is everything. The documents are not processed in the normal sense of the word.

- **Customer versus user orientation.** By its very nature, this model is dominantly customer oriented. The whole idea is to facilitate access to any one or any set of related references.

- **Processing.** In this model, processing is mostly interactive searching—adding and deleting documents from the system.

- **Relatability.** Arguably, relatability is dominant in this model. The idea is to be able to take a topic or its equivalent and explore the various paths that lead from it. The use of this feature varies with the circumstances.

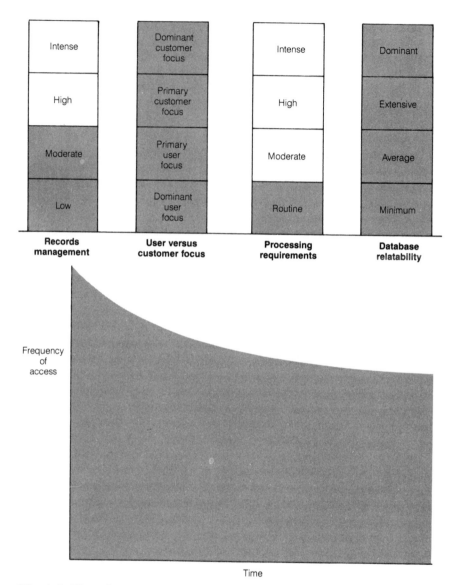

Records management	User versus customer focus	Processing requirements	Database relatability
Intense	Dominant customer focus	Intense	Dominant
High	Primary customer focus	High	Extensive
Moderate	Primary user focus	Moderate	Average
Low	Dominant user focus	Routine	Minimum

Frequency of access

Time

Fig. A-3. The reference model is essentially an automated library with facsimile document storage—not just the computer-based index systems commonly found in libraries today.

- **Access requirements versus time.** The reference model essentially mandates the fastest possible access times. Many documents might have to be perused before the search pays off.

- **Opportunities.** In the long view, the opportunities could almost be described as extreme. For example, the United States uses artificial intelligence to process patent applications, which is already stored in an image system.

A.4 Document-generation model

The document-generation model is an outgrowth of automated publishing and goes beyond the occasional need to generate intermediate and output documents in other models (FIG. A-4). The generation itself is the reason for creating the system. Earlier automated publishing systems concentrated on text files. So, editorial matter could be developed in locations worldwide, consolidated in editorial offices, and the resulting pages would be distributed to many printing plants concurrently. All of the major news magazines and the *Wall Street Journal* use this process. Imaging extends it to all documents that cannot be readily reduced to text files (e.g. engineering drawings and geographically-oriented management systems). The difference from the reference model is that the documents are used to generate additional documents or at least updates to the existing files.

- **Records management.** In volume, the workload can be massive, but from a structural perspective, it is little different than the reference model.

- **Customer versus user orientation.** This ratio varies with the application. It can be intensely customer oriented or used primarily for the convenience of the immediate users.

- **Processing.** Processing can range from negligible to intense, depending on what is produced and what input is available. Digitizing existing hardcopy engineering drawings into a CAD (computer assisted drafting) file for subsequent modification is a classic example of complex processing.

- **Relatability.** Strong relatability within the folder of documents for a specific file, which can number in the tens of thousands, is indispensable, but the interfolder relatability requirements are fewer.

- **Access requirements versus time.** Unless the system is dominantly customer oriented, most users can tolerate minor delays in access. However, this should not be confused with the rapid access times appropriate for a system that is more reference oriented than document-generation oriented.

- **Opportunities.** In a sense, this model already exemplifies the advantages that are offered by image technology.

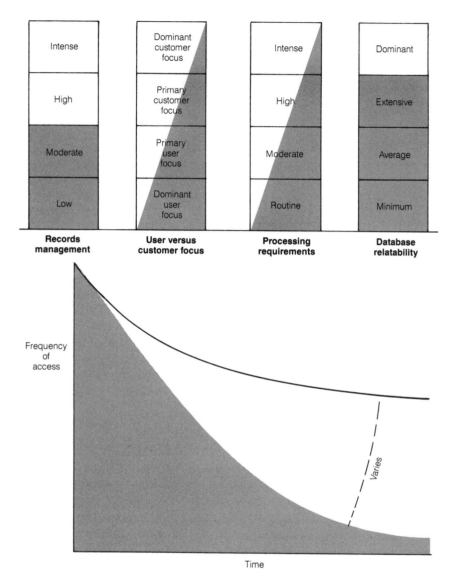

Fig. A-4. The document-generation model tends to superimpose the reference model with automated publishing and is used extensively by a wide range of newspapers and periodicals as well as engineering firms.

Appendix B

Case examples

Everybody wants to get into the act.
Jimmy Durante

The 18 case examples cited in this appendix have been selected for several reasons. First, these cases involve many different vendors. Second, they represent different applications. Third, with one exception (which will be the largest in the world), they are all operational installations, even though many are in the process of expanding into additional phases. Fourth, they cover both profit and non-profit applications. Fifth, each has been documented in published material (albeit provided by vendors in a few cases). Sixth, they include two instances of reliance on micrographics in favor of electronic imaging.

It should be noted, however, that existing installations already number in the thousands. It is therefore impossible to select a truly representative sample or even to do full justice to the few systems that are included. For readers who want a more detailed review of selected cases, the third binder volume in *Document Image Processing* (listed in the references) is a good source that includes many successful systems in other countries.

The reader might also be skeptical about to the apparent success of nearly every system on record. That is hard to believe, but so far that is what the facts indicate. However, not all systems have generated the anticipated investment return as soon as planned. Some required a few more months to reach the break-even point.

B.1 USAA (IBM)

USAA is a diversified insurance and financial management company that is headquartered in San Antonio, Texas. Its approximately 2 million-member client base consists primarily of active, retired, former officers of the armed forces, and (by way of a subsidiary) the grown former dependents of members who would otherwise not be eligible for membership. It is the sixth-largest insurer of automobiles and homes in the United States and the largest direct-response life insurer in the world. It was also one of the first companies to strive for a "paperless" environment—long before image processing became commercially available.

The "paperless" challenge was offered by the chief executive officer, retired Air Force Brigadier General Robert F. McDermott at a meeting in January 1969.[1] Because of the lack of suitable, affordable technology, 12 years were required to convert this challenge into a workable report. An interim experiment with micrographics failed in the sense that the inconvenience of retrieving film images outweighed the cost savings.

In the mid-1980s, electronic image facsimile prototypes from 3M and FileNet were tried and developed over the next several years with great success. However, at the time the products were nonstandard. USAA wanted a system that was built from standardized elements or elements that would become standard. The primary reason was that the system for property insurance and claims would use at least one thousand terminals (many thousand for all its operations). Also, USAA wanted to keep open the option of distributing at least part of the system to other processing locations. Custom-built systems rarely afford flexibility.

Accordingly, requests for information were sent to vendors in early 1987. Of those that responded, IBM won the contract in July 1987, and within 11 months, announced the arrival of their MVS ImagePlus system. The much larger system worked well and provided the springboard for IBM to become the largest single vendor of image systems in just two years. The USAA project became a critical milestone in the history of information and image processing.

The details of this system are too complex to fully summarize in two pages, and moreover, some of the specifics worked out for USAA might not be exportable "as is" to other organizations. Nevertheless, several points are worth noting from a cost and management viewpoint.

- **Space and personnel.** Roughly 39 thousand square feet of paper file storage space was reduced to 100 square feet with image processing and 120 personnel were reassigned to "more meaningful" jobs.

- **Productivity.** USAA estimated that the system reduced the number of professionals using the system by between 2 and 10 percent, which

---

[1]Sources: C.A. Plesums and R.W. Bartels, "Large scale systems: USAA case study," *IBM Systems Journal*, Vol. 29, No. 3, 1990, 343-355 and Charles A. Plesums, "Image Processing at USAA," *Mainframe Journal*, June 1990, 8-15. The former article is longer and provides more technical detail on the USAA system.

translates (for USAA) into a savings of approximately one million dollars per year per percentage point.

• **Integration.** Prior to implementing of this system, USAA invested $100 million revamping its applications programs. Therefore, it was essential that the imaging would be integrated with this programming while making the integration appear "seamless" to users. The effort succeeded, but arguably only because this requirement was taken into account from the beginning of the image project.

• **Indexing and initial processing.** USAA tried several options and then settled on "manually" entering a key index value on each document before scanning it in their mailroom. Thus, an interactive screen is generated for subsequent, minimum-possible input of any necessary data after scanning. It was found that a mere 50 index/document codes covered 95% of the input volume, and only the last 5% required one of several hundred other codes. This had a significant impact on the acquisition operation and training procedures.

• **Image resolution.** Image files demand enormous memory, so it is tempting to settle on the lowest possible resolution that will meet "most requirements." One hundred pixels per inch will do this, but the USAA concluded that such a criterion wasn't good enough; it should be "all requirements." As such, they elected to scan at 200 pixels per inch.

• **Computer-generated raster images.** Superimposition of text data over imaged forms for output (such as policies) and to save that image as a vector (rather than a raster-type) image is used extensively. This greatly reduced storage requirements for the file copies, offsetting the cost of scanning at 200-pixels-per-inch for input documents.

B.2 Northwest Airlines (Andersen Consulting with a FileNet system)[2]

Most airlines are faced with a problem that was insurmountable before image processing became available. Airlines cannot process the mass of ticket and reservation data fast enough to accurately set and reset ticket prices, routes, and to make other decisions in the highly competitive arena of deregulated passenger air traffic. The situation is vaguely similar to a pari-mutual racetrack that cannot recompute the odds until after each race is over. For Northwest Airlines, the fourth largest airline in the United States, the numbers were

---

[2]Source: An Image of the Future: Northwest Airlines and FileNet Integrate Imaging into Mission-Critical Revenue System, FileNet Corporation, Costa Mesa, California, 1990.

so staggering that they had to rely on statistical sampling to derive any kind of workable parameters.

The company processes 600 million transactions per year, derived from 60 thousand agents, which involve interline transfers with approximately 200 other airlines worldwide. Of this total, 10 percent are sales and use documents (equal to 5 million per month) compounded by constant price changes, variable commissions to agents, refunds to passengers, and numerous corrections. Even these magnitudes could have been tamed by data processing. However, the data originates from three disparate sources that are difficult to conventionally integrate: the electronic sales record in the reservation system, paper records from the selling sources (audit coupons), and the tickets collected at airport gates (flight coupons).

Because the reservation data alone was in good shape, the key was to include OCR reduction of the ticket and stock control numbers while also making an image record of each ticket. Once scanned, all records are logically consolidated and accessible for follow-on processing. The digitized ticket data solved the integration problem and the electronic image files ushered in the productivity advantages of image processing.

When corrections are necessary, operators can instantly retrieve all appropriate documentation on screen (using windows-type software): the applicable digitally-stored data (audit data), ticket sale information, and the ticket itself. Any disconnects are spotted instantly and corrected. It has paid for itself by way of its much better handle on pricing, which has improved profits while improving service, and also by the "traditional" image-processing savings in space, personnel, and productivity.

B.3 Rolls-Royce and Associates Ltd.[3] (Unisys beta test)

Rolls-Royce and Associates Ltd. (RRA) a wholly owned subsidiary of Rolls-Royce that builds pressurized reactors for England's fleet of nuclear submarines, has recently made its services available for commercial customers. Like all elements of Rolls-Royce, it pays meticulous attention to inventories and engineering drawings, but some problems are beyond the reach of the most dedicated. The shear number of parts and drawings is too large to manage and the paper used in many applications is onion-thin and it begins to deteriorate after 30 years or so.

The original solution was limited to a relational database index system, the Parts Information Management System (PIMS), to keep tabs on inventory. About the time this came on line, Unisys decided to develop and market image systems. Since RRA was an established Unisys customer, they were asked to

---

[3]Source: Ted Rasch, "Building a Better Beta at Rolls Royce," *Inform*, October 1990, 26-28.

serve as the beta test site for engineering applications. The skepticism at first was noticeable, but the price was right and Unisys promised to insure the system. However, it would eventually shape up and change the direction of RRI's requirements.

As the test proceeded, however, officials on both sides began to see the synergetic relationship between automated parts inventory and engineering drawings. The former system often required access to the records of the latter. But the major surprise was the enormous cost savings that resulted from the InfoImage system.

The main opportunity arose with the necessity to convert older drawings to CAD systems, even though the drawings probably would not be modified. The nature of nuclear power requires that these drawings are kept in meticulous condition. Ron Hawley, manager of the drawing office and project manager for the system, said, "We exist through documentation." Image processing solved the problem.

Another interesting aspect of this system was the ability to integrate hardware from different vendors, including mainframes from Unisys, Microvax minicomputers from Digital Equipment Corporation, and personal computers from Sun Microsystems. Hawley's objective was to incorporate the image system as an element in a much larger information system, not the driver. Unisys accomplished the task.

B.4 Additional engineer[4] document management systems

Probably the largest engineer document management system in the United States is being developed for the U.S. Navy's Engineering Data Management Information and Control System, EDMICS. It is a burden to shore management and increasingly an impossibility for copies to be maintained at sea.

This system is being developed under a 10-year contract with Advanced Technology. The subcontractors include the Eastman Kodak Company, Digital Equipment Corporation, Formteck, Inc., Sun Microsystems, Wicks and Wilson U.S.A., Xerox Corporation, and Zenith Data Systems Corporation. The initial unit is being installed at the Naval Ordinance Station at Louisville, Kentucky, and it is the first of 47 planned units at 43 different facilities. The system replaces a largely manual system that used conventional records, CAD, and micrographics.

EDMICS will not be as large as the system designed for the IRS (section B.8), but arguably it is more complex and the records are subject to millions of unique updates. Some operating specifications are tough: engineering drawings that comprise millions of bytes must be retrievable under 10 seconds, and batch scanners must process four existing aperture cards per second.

---

[4]Sources: Gregory E. Kaebnick, "EDMICS Goes to Work," *Inform*, October 1990, 15-18, and Michael Pennington, "Colorado Springs Takes a Good Look at Itself," same issue, 22-26.

Unfortunately, space limitations do not permit even a good executive over-view of EDMICS in this book. If any doubt exists that image processing will become the dominant form for processing within 10 years, this project should dispel it.

The Department of Utilities for Colorado Springs, Colorado, chose micro-form over electronic imaging. The requirements were important, but the mag-nitudes did not justify a more expensive image system. Those requirements involved direct management of the four common utilities: gas, electricity, water, and waste water. Map books were converted to aperture cards using 3M equipment. Updates are common, but micrographics technology is at the point where they can be made in a reasonable time frame and the copies can be dis-tributed to the departments that need them. Because of the nature of the work, instant updates are not required. New gas lines are not laid that quickly.

B.5 An integrated system (IBM)[5]

The Office of Motor Vehicles for the state of Louisiana, demonstrates the wide range of potential for the integration with image systems.

In particular, Louisiana has a reputation for the aggressive use of auto-mated data processing systems. Rex McDonald, the undersecretary for Public Safety and Corrections (employing seven thousand people) said "we're con-stantly automating projects." Accordingly, the 1,400 terminals and the annual load of 12 million documents (in view of the emergence of image processing) mandated attention to integration. This department was also one of the first to recognize the potential of imaging, and in 1986, successfully advocated pas-sage of a state law that allowed digitized image records (of fingerprints ini-tially) as evidence in court.

By 1988, they were ready for a more extensive use of imaging. The prob-lem was that their data processing systems were hosted on mainframes manu-factured by a vendor that had not yet entered the image market. IBM had, but their ImagePlus systems are intended for IBM host computers. Nevertheless, IBM invested 1,200 manhours analyzing the situation, and developed the nec-essary software to link their image solution and IBM computer with data proc-essing running on a computer from another vendor and thus ensured image and conventional databases could be accessed in tandem. The system has been expanded considerably since that time, and it now makes maximum use of automated indexing and optical character recognition.

In more detail, the key component was the file folder facility. McDonald said, "What we're beginning to do is shift considerable resources from main-taining and filing data to an end-user solution. The folder application facility brought us a substantial change in allowing you to control your work load as well as presenting you with the image of the original documents."

---

[5]Sources: Ted Rasch, "Imaging in the Big Easy," *Inform*, November/December 1990, 14-16.

He went on to explain how the system for rotating documents was pegged to specific employee skills, which is similar to the USAA setup (Case Study B-1). He also noted that virtually no data was lost or destroyed when IBM linked its system with the databases stored on Unisys computers.

B.6 Three Eastman Kodak systems[6]

Eastman Kodak is not in the computer business, but it has been in the image business for more than a century. It makes optical disks, jukeboxes, scanners, printers, software and many other elements associated with image systems. The three installations summarized in this section illustrate the diversity of this technology.

The system at SmithKline Beecham Pharmaceuticals demonstrates a clear strategic advantage gained by imaging. Now drugs can be brought to the marketplace faster with the side benefit of saving millions of dollars in research and development costs. In clinical trials, the physicians who participate in the testing of new drugs record patient reactions on company-supplied forms. These forms, of course, are returned and then must be collated, compiled, reviewed, and otherwise managed in dozen of ways to assess the effects of the drugs at issue. It's a paperwork nightmare and image processing offered an ideal solution.

With this system, forms are precoded with OCR data that is digitized when scanned (with 98 percent accuracy in the first pass alone). This data, which includes the form number, drug name, patient number, and protocol number (not to be confused with network communication protocols), is then automatically entered into a relational database index. Another feature permits the generation of image overlays that operators use to translate the often (and traditional, it seems) illegible handwriting without changing anything else on the original document.

From that point, improvement to evaluation productivity skyrockets, to include faxing images back to the participating physicians when necessary— often just to add comments or to answer questions that arise after the returns are tabulated. This way, documents are not lost and they can be processed concurrently. Further, each analyst is ensured of access to the most current data. True, all of this could have been accomplished manually, but it would have entailed unacceptably high costs and an oppressive supervisory regime.

The second system has fewer strategic goals, but its effects are just as important. This unit automated the aircraft maintenance records for Continental Airlines. Continental has 334 aircraft and 50 maintenance stations worldwide. Good maintenance means fewer mishaps; that saves lives.

The problem is that some maintenance for each aircraft is performed at designated stations, but some of it must be done wherever the problems occur.

---

[6]Sources: Material provided by Eastman Kodak.

Moreover, aircraft must often be transferred to support changing flight schedules and passenger traffic. Also, the average aircraft lasts about 25 years, is often retrofitted with new technology, and is subject to changing maintenance requirements.

As such, it is easy to lose track of maintenance records, to omit critical work, or to repeat work already done. Moreover, the Federal Aviation Administration (FAA) inspectors assume that when records do not exist or cannot be located, the maintenance was not performed. These mistakes lead to stiff fines and eventually a bad reputation—even if the airline is lucky enough to avoid crashes.

This system, which allows operators to enter up to 16 index fields, can instantly access any number of record combinations to meet any number of requirements. This system connects seven million documents to more than one thousand terminals from the Kodak Image Management System to the company's mainframe computer. Never, never underestimate the utility of a relational database—neither for traditional data processing nor as an image system index.

The third system in this set is even more mundane; it concentrates almost solely on the basic advantages of image processing. It encompasses the operations at the Exchange National Bank in suburban Chicago, Illinois, and is a classic example of developing a comprehensive plan at the enterprise level and then implementing each department in a scheduled sequence.

The initial phase began in the credit department, which had grown to cover an intolerable amount of floor space. Also, too many documents could not be found in time to react to inquiries and problems. Fortunately, the image system worked so well that the next phases are being implemented as soon as possible on the demand-deposit account files and the 30 thousand American Express Gold Card files. Even these relatively small applications will save $30,000 per year in storage space.

B.7 Four Wang Laboratories systems[7]

Four installations covered in this section all use the Wang Integrated Image Systems (WIIS) or at least variations derived from it. The first of these is a legal image information system developed for the Howrey and Simon law firm in Washington, D.C. (a long-time Wang customer), and is a very good example of applying relational database index logic to a growing reference system. The system, the Litigation Imaging and Information System (LIIS), uses PACE database software.

Tens of thousands of documents must be accessed and cross referenced in different combinations to support different cases. As the number of documents increases, the scope of the problem increases exponentially until it

---

[7]Source: A Comprehensive Guide to Integrated Image Systems, Wang Laboratories, Lowell, Massachusetts, 1990.

becomes unmanageable. That is precisely what happened at Howrey and Simon. So, they installed a relational database index system in the late 1970s. This system did relieve some of the problem, but the increasing mass of paper records had a tendency to negate the advantages. Wang later developed an image system for the law firm (and hence the integration of imaging and database software), that eliminated the paperwork bottlenecks.

The second system was installed at a departmental level for the City of Eindhoven (The Netherlands) for building permits. The rationale was to harness the image system to distribute copies of the same folder to separate administrative sections into environmental, financial, legal, and planning departments. Also, the building-permit process in a European city is much more detailed and tedious than in America.

The installation also provides insight into the problem of trying to use concurrent processing when sequential processing is absolutely necessary. The solution is deceptively simple—don't try to make it concurrent. A file can be instantly transferred from one department (as soon as their work is finished) to the queue of the next department in the sequence. Priority codes can be automatically upgraded, if appropriate.

The third system was an internal accounting project for McDonnell Douglas, headquartered in St. Louis, Missouri. This system processes invoices from its vendors (to include the supporting documentation), debit and credit memos, check requests, small cash transactions, and other familiar accounting functions.

The advantages, as enumerated in the Wang Laboratories reference, are: documents are indexed to business-related key words to pave the way for tailor-made searches, documents are automatically routed to appropriate departments for processing based on the transaction codes, necessary audit trail information is created, critical management information reports (both for the system itself and for the purposes to which the system is put) are generated, and workstations can display different images and data from different sources on the same screen.

In addition to the obvious gains in direct productivity and document control, McDonnell Douglas found that it had much more control over accounting work, which in turn has led to higher profits. Perhaps these advantages are available from all image systems, but not every company has elected to do so. Some companies do not always install the system with maximum efficiency in mind.

The fourth system was a tracking-and-locator project for the American Red Cross. What formerly required six months now whips along at an average of two weeks. The reason for the delays was simply that 90 percent of the necessary research sources comprised photographs, handwritten letters, and fingerprints that were not easy to digitally process.*

---

*This is not quite true in theory for fingerprints, but it takes a major agency, such as the Federal Bureau of Investigation, to complete these projects economically.

The existing manual system had grown to 800 thousand index cards for 200 thousand cases filed. That might seem like slim pickings for a commercial image processing system, but not when the work entails human "scanning" of several thousand documents to solve just one case. The task is arguably more difficult than, say, processing a patent application. Moreover, paper records can easily be transferred to sites where the expertise exists to analyze them. Little details (like what part of a name is considered the "last name" differs with cultures) can wreak havoc on a search when they are performed by an individual who is unfamiliar with the cultural traditions that are applicable to the case. The upshot is that refugees can now be reunited with their families much more quickly.

B.8 Two legal systems (FileNet)[8]

Although the Northwest Airlines system described in B.2 is of high significance, it was not planned and developed by FileNet itself. That is misleading because this company has installed approximately 335 systems to date. Two of those are summarized here; both are court-oriented to illustrate the extent to which imaging can be used.

The new two-person carpool express lanes on the Los Angeles freeways have provided an opportunity for drivers to create a new brand of humor—if they are willing to pay the minimum price of $248 per quip. Hearse drivers have tried to claim their horizontal occupants meet the prerequisite for at least one passenger, as have pregnant women with respect to their unborn children (although an individual who takes a baby to a daycare center on the way to work does qualify to use the lanes).

Unfortunately, processing the volume of traffic citations in Southern California (which exceeds one million per year) is no joke. Enter image processing. Both Los Angeles and Santa Monica have installed these systems to rid themselves of the mass of paper that is associated with tickets, warrants, and related documents. This efficiency passes on to both the courts and the drivers. The drivers, when they want to settle or contest their cases, no longer have to wait while harried clerks attempt to find the necessary documents. In many cases, the paperwork would have been sent on to a courtroom, misfiled, or just simply lost. Moreover, this system permits many of these transactions to be conducted over the telephone. The waiting time to retrieve the records has been reduced to a few seconds. The system hasn't been linked to any credit card companies yet, but that would be a logical step.

---

[8]Source: Materials provided to the author by the FileNet Corporation. FileNet also offers a detailed videotape that illustrates how the system works.

The system has also introduced a new improvement to productivity—one that was not entirely welcomed by some holders of traffic citations. The automation of the documentation, and the necessary indexes, also means that outstanding warrants would be processed more readily and that scofflaws would be hauled into court more often and faster than in previous times. Also, the revenues increased for the city and the system began to pay for itself from this source—as well as from the savings in personnel and space. In time, the index data might be used so that the police can better manage automobile traffic.

The second installation is also court-based, but this time it is for the probate in the Orange County Superior Court. In the words of FileNet, this system is used "to streamline the time-consuming chore of filing and subsequently locating thousands of legal documents each month and distributing them to the multitude of court files and to paralegal probate examiners for review in advance of court hearings," which "will allow the simultaneous review of the same document or file by many different people, including court personnel, attorneys and litigants." In this case, concurrent processing is the rule, not the exception.

This system replaces the "laundry carts" (filled with wills, guardianships, conservatorships, trusts, and other probate documents) that have been in use since the 1950s. It has 40 terminal workstations, including two for the presiding probate judge. He has one in his chambers and one on the bench!

According to the court's chief executive officer, Alan Slater, this system is the first of its kind in a United States court of general jurisdiction, and was really intended as a prototype for much larger operations. The reasoning was that probate is a microcosm of all the processes that occur in both civil and criminal courts. Incidentally, this is a rare case when a working installation also serves as a genuine prototype.

What's more, this system serves as a model for other courts at local, state, and federal levels. Using a grant of approximately $120 thousand from the Federal State Justice Institute, the National Center for State Courts is conducting and will publish a study and cost-benefit analysis on the impact of image systems on court operations. The study will cover staffing, work flow, records management, and other areas of interest.

However, this particular system is anything but a model in size. The upfront costs were in the vicinity of $1.3 million (one of the few publicly disclosed prices for specific systems) and includes approximately 8,500 active probate files comprising about 844 thousand pages. Any page can be retrieved within 15 seconds, assuming the operator or user has the correct index information. If not, the on-line index can be scanned until the correct entry is found.

This installation has improved productivity and saved taxpayer dollars, but the real significance is that courts are moving towards a so-called "paperless" environment. So, the legal obstacles to accepting image documents as evidence (chapter 9) will fade, at least in part. The judge, so to speak, has become a friend of the court.

B.9 The Federal Internal[9] Revenue Service project

Obviously, the Internal Revenue Service processes more paperwork than any other organization in the world. What's more, a good slice of those documents must be kept in semi-active status for 50 years or more. The IRS also transacts more funds than any other agency in the world, save the Treasury (the immediate recipient of the IRS funds output).

The situation is further compounded by the intensity of the traffic. Roughly 200 million forms (75% are income tax returns in some form) are received each year, most of them in a two month period, and refunds must be mailed within 45 days. That requirement arises from the need to audit and also to ensure processing quality control at the front end. That is, audits are generally conducted after the main filing season and this requires access to millions of documents stored in processing centers, and that can take four to six weeks. Moreover, it is not practical to earmark all of these records at the time of processing. Additionally, the image processing would have the side benefit of speeding up front-end processing and thus improving customer service.

Therefore, the IRS initiated the Files Archival Image Storage and Retrieval (FAISR) program as a research test in January 1983—two years *before* FileNet installed the first standard image system. In May 1984, the contract was awarded to Integrated Automation in Alameda, California. The test was conducted at the Fresno district office, from late 1985 to the end of 1987. The summary report was issued in 1988. True, five years might seem like a long time, but this prototype applied technology in its infancy to the largest document processing system in the world, which at the time was also having its data processing system revamped. Still, the lessons learned osmosed throughout the image processing industry.

The chief of these lessons focused on the severe limitations that would be imposed by any closed architecture system, especially when access to image records had to be integrated with existing data processing systems. Accordingly, the FAISR system itself was dismantled and sent to the National Bureau of Standards for more research. Additionally, many other technical issues surfaced, not the least of which was the problem of memory-hungry high-resolution and graytone image requirements. Happily, subsequent vendor sensitivity to these problems have made them almost academic. The same cannot be said of the management-oriented problems that were summarized in the remarkably candid IRS after-action report. The IRS resolved them for itself, but most of these problems continue to crop up in other installations. And this is in keeping with the general agreement among professionals that for the time being at least, the accelerating interest in imaging is outpacing the available

---

[9]Source: Final Report: Files Archival Image Storage and Retrieval (FAISR), September 26, 1988, and Document Processing System, May 7, 1990, both published by the Internal Revenue Service.

expertise. The points noted by the IRS were:

- **Contracting personnel.** If the personnel who are responsible for developing a systems agreement are unfamiliar with image processing, and the intended system involves new features (at least with respect to the vendor's experience), then unless the users are fully consulted, the agreement will fail and the users will informally modify the agreement that exists to the point of creating major problems.

- **Project staff.** The IRS admitted that some of the problems noted in its report would not have occurred had the prototype staff been more fully staffed, and with the correct mix of expertise, especially in ADP.

- **Specificity and documentation.** The agreement lacked specificity and the vendor did not provide sufficient documentation as the system was being developed. As a result, software costs jumped unnecessarily—especially with respect to performance standards and testing, despite the experimental nature of the project.

- **Progress meetings and reports.** Progress meetings and reports were infrequent and resulted in major misunderstandings between the vendor and the IRS. These misunderstandings led to design decisions that ignored requirements. Sound familiar?

- **Vendor's technical expertise and understanding of requirements.** The IRS took responsibility for not ensuring the vendor had the best available experience for the job and for not fully educating him on the exceedingly complex requirements once the agreement was signed.

Despite these problems, and perhaps because the IRS was willing to take a hard and honest look at the results of the prototype, it spent several years refining explicit requirements for an initial installation at the district processing center in Austin, Texas. In January 1991, IBM was awarded the $342 million dollar contract.

B.10 Micrographics at the Utah State Tax Commission[10]

Image processing has not displaced micrographics, and much is to be said for modernizing existing micrographics systems, rather than replacing them with electronic imaging. Utah offers a case in point, and offers an interesting contrast to the IRS for the same requirements—albeit with less than one percent

---

[10]Source: James L. Rhodes, "Utah Upgrade," *Inform*, November/December 1990, 8-12.

of the volume. This load consisted of roughly 15 thousand rolls of 16mm microfilm stored in 47 file cabinets that used about 425 square feet of office space. The problem was retrieval time. The criterion was two days, but in practice it often required three to six days and seasonal employees had to help with the peak loads of 12 thousand requests per month. The solution was to automate microfilm retrieval.

The first step was to adapt relational database concepts to labeling the rolls of microfilm so that they did not have to be stored in a specific sequence. The next step was to automate this indexing system. Then, all of the film was placed in automated carousel-type storage cabinets (each roll placed in an ANSI-standard "C" clip for quick access). This completed the first phase of the modernization.

The second phase involved an extension to convert existing paperwork to micrographics storage. Approximately 200 thousand folders had to be labeled, bar coded, indexed, and in many cases, cross-referenced. Kardex (who also supplied the carousels) wrote the custom software required and the equipment to fully automate this will be provided by Eastman Kodak. The requests processed per month have increased from 12 thousand to 16 thousand with a turnaround time of only one day, without any seasonal staffing. The Tax Commission also expects to cut the number of terminal operators from seven to five.

Still, much is to be said for electronic image processing, and the Commission plans to add it later for the most intensely accessed documents. In doing so, they will rely on Kodak's successful technology to integrate the computer-assisted retrieval (CAR) of micrographics images and the digital kind.

Appendix C
Technical Notes

Bungling fools!

One scientist to another, in an old
movie, after being informed that
a nuclear explosion set in the
arctic had put the earth on a
collision course with the sun.

This appendix explains the mechanics for a number of technical points of significance to decisionmakers. Image technology is more complex than implied
in this appendix, but it does not affect the underlying principles.

C.1 Miscellaneous imaging factors

In theory, many factors can affect how documents in an image system are
scanned, stored, displayed, or printed. In practice, only a few of them can be
used to reduce storage length, and the potential savings are often offset by the
need for more sophisticated hardware.

- **Discrete versus addressable resolution.** A common feature of
  some printers, especially 24-pin dot-matrix printers, is to overlap dots in
  order to provide smoother images. As such, the addressable dots or pixels are not the same as discrete pixels (FIG. C-1).
- **Aspect ratio and scaling.** The *aspect ratio* is the ratio of the horizontal pixels per unit of measurement to the number of lines (rasters) of pixels for the same unit of measurement vertically. *Scaling* is the process of
  changing the aspect ratio of an image so that either the horizontal or the
  vertical dimension is exaggerated. The significance is that scaling can
  occur with printers if the controls are incorrectly set with respect to the
  image records.
- **Continuous tone ranges.** The shades of gray produced by pixel data
  in a continuous tone image record is 2 raised to a power equal to the
  number of bits (per pixel) minus 2. Thus, an 8-bit pixel produces 254

165

Discrete *equals* addressable resolution
Each printed dot stands in its own unique space.

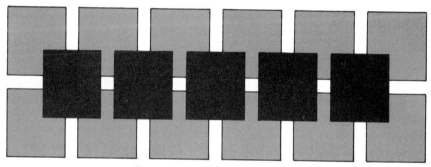

Discrete *less than* addressable resolution
Printed dots overlap and are no longer individually distinguishable.

Fig. C-1. When the dots or pixels of an image overlap to create the appearance of smoother edges, the discrete resolution is less than the addressable resolution—even though the record must store the larger number of pixels.

intermediate tones. Because the human eye can distinguish only about 125 shades (at best), it would appear that storage lengths could be reduced by lopping a bit off every byte. Unfortunately, computer hardware is designed to work with powers of 2 (2,4,8,16, etc) and it is therefore impractical. The practical choice is 14 intermediate shades or 254 shades and the latter takes only twice the storage space.

- **Compression versus reduction.** *Reduction* refers to the shrinking of an image, normally in proportion. *Compression* reorganizes the bitstream in order to reduce its length for storage purposes. Only uncompressed or decompressed images can be reduced or enlarged. Reducing an image before compression will reduce the record length (if the same scanning resolution is used) because there will be fewer pixels to scan.

However, the resolution will be poorer when that image is decompressed and enlarged back to its original size. The same effect can be achieved by just lowering the resolution.

- **Mixed or compound images.** A *mixed* or *compound image* uses different techniques to store (and display) different areas of a single image. If an image consists of a photo and text, the entire image could be scanned as a graytone, or the photo can be scanned in graytone and the text as a bilevel. Sophisticated scanners and algorithms are required to do this, but it can significantly reduce storage requirements.

- **Three-dimensional images.** Although it is not commonly used in commercial image processing systems, each pixel can also include additional data to specify the distance of the dot that is represented by that pixel from a fixed plane. Thus, a true three-dimensional image can be produced in a holograph projection system or it can be used as input data in a vector image analysis model.

C.2 Optical character recognition

Optical character recognition is a special type of pattern recognition. The shape or configuration of a character or symbol is matched with a library of symbols, each of which has either a standard ASCII code number or a user-designated code. When a match is found, that code is recorded as part of the record bitstream.

OCR is therefore related to mark sense forms and bar codes. To the computer or scanner, the letter "R" is in the same league as ▮▮ ▮▮▮ . Both are patterns. The only thing that it cares about, so to speak, is that the patterns are used consistently, and that they always match an entry in the pattern library. More precisely, it requires the patterns to be different enough that the minor variations of the same pattern are negligible compared to the differences among patterns.

Standard OCR characters and bar codes provide a nearly ideal environment. The software required to interpret anything less than that standard rise exponentially, as shown in FIG. C-2. If different sizes are used, the algorithm must be able to reduce or enlarge (or compute the ratios) each pattern until a match is found. When typewriter/printer fonts are used, many different pattern sets must be maintained in a library. Moreover, the scanner must first determine which font was used. Fortunately, a mere six fonts account for 98 percent of all printed material.

When the material is handprinted or scribed, then current algorithms come apart at the seams (FIG. C-2). True, some printing and writing is easier to decipher than others, but any system intended to scan documents must be prepared to accept and process all but the absolute worst cases (which would have

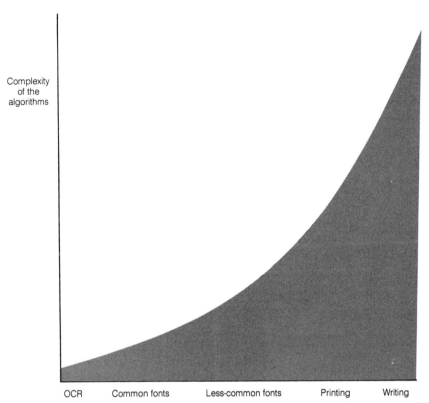

Fig. C-2. As characters targeted for pattern recognition progress to handwritten and scribbled notes, the complexity of the algorithms required increases exponentially.

to be scanned as standard raster images). To understand the challenge, consider what happens when the human eye encounters fuzzy writing. All the powers of the brain bear on the tiny problem of a string of five to ten characters. It sometimes takes minutes to decipher a single word.

OCR must create a pattern recognition chart for each document (or template one from a library), recognize variations, follow stray writing up and down hill, ignore any printed lines and "noise" that the writing might intersect, and accommodate variations in the same character in the same document. Some of this will eventually be accomplished. Strong economic incentives drive the research, not only for image systems but also for organizations such as the postal service.

However, no matter how functional these algorithms become, some writing will always remain illegible. Some parts should not be reduced to text (e.g., signatures). Therefore, the use of OCR for handwriting—technically called *neural OCR (NOCR)*—will always be subject to trade-offs. Moreover, certain documents must be retained in raster form—anything less reliable would not stand in court.

The alternative of using manual verification for each document would more than likely be a prohibitive expense. Thus, the real payoff for NOCR might be recording printed matter for image libraries. In that situation, print-font OCR can be used—almost always without concerns for court standing.

C.3 Compression and decompression algorithms

Compression algorithms trade bytes for bits (FIG. C-3). At first glance that seems to be a bad bargain, because a byte typically has 8 bits. The saving grace is that a byte can store numbers up to 256 and 2-byte units (a word) can accommodate numbers as high as 65,535. The simplest case is the raster of pixels that is blank. If the paper is 8½ inches wide and the resolution is 200 pixels per inch, 200 bytes (1,600 bits) are required to store it. However, if stretches of either one color or the other (in bilevel images) were recorded as data, then a single 2-byte unit (16 bits) plus an end-of-line indicator would do the trick. If 1-byte units were used, a maximum of 7 bytes of storage (1,600/ 256 = 6.25 rounded to 7) and the end-of-line indicator would be required.

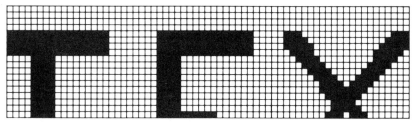

Text-based image. Changes from foreground to background color occur infrequently relative to the number of pixels, and therefore the common compression algorithms work efficiently. Equivalent record lengths are reduced by a factor between 10 and 20.

Picture-based image. By contrast, the changes from foreground to background color (or vice versa) are much more frequent than in a text-based image, and thus the byte (compressed image) is worse than the bark (the uncompressed image as a cover of rasters).

Fig. C-3. Compression algorithms substitute numbers (with one or two bytes) for segments of identical pixels (in lieu of recording each one as a bit). The trade-off is super for text, but break even, at best, for pictures.

In a worst-case situation, where each raster consisted of an alternating set of data (i.e., on and off), the technique would bankrupt the system. The 1-byte unit algorithm would eat 1,600 bytes and the 2-byte unit would eat 3,200 bytes. If the document was 11 inches long, 3,520,000 bytes would be required for the 1-byte unit, and twice that for the 2-byte unit (see FIG. C-3).

Where is the trade-off? The answer depends on three factors: resolution, whether each line is computed as an entity versus being recorded only as it changes from the previous line (the FAX standard), whether 2-byte or 1-byte data units are used, and to a much lesser extent, whether end-of-line indicators are included or if the counting process wraps like a word processor.

Fortunately, extensive mathematical analyses of this kind are seldom necessary. For the most part, text-oriented images fall well below the trade-off point and most picture-oriented images occur way above it. Therefore the scanner only needs to compare the compressed bitstream length with the uncompressed. If it is significantly less, the compressed image should be stored. If not, the original bitstream should be annotated as uncompressed and then stored in that format.

Without this decision, a system must either record all images in compressed form or all in uncompressed form. However, unless the vast majority of documents was one type or the other, the storage capacity would soon be overtaxed, especially for text-oriented images. These techniques might all sound tedious, of course, but the length of stored records exerts such an overwhelming influence on system capital and operating costs that managers concentrate on available economies.

Compression algorithms for picture-oriented images are available, but work by sacrificing some degree of authenticity (called *lossy*). These algorithms are based on the following logic. Start with a section of an image, say, 8 × 8 bits, and use a 1-byte pixel for continuous tone. It takes 64 bytes to record, so 6.277 * 1057 patterns can occur within that section. More than 99 percent of the patterns that do occur number no more than 64 thousand. Thus, any one of those 64 thousand patterns can be logged with a 2-byte number. Voila, 64 bytes of raster image is reduced to 2 bytes—usually with only minimal loss to authenticity (the 64 thousand patterns have a certain stretch to accommodate minor variations).

C.4 Optical disk technology

Optical disks use technology similar to phonograph records, albeit with a sophistication and refinement that is incomparable in terms of quality. With analog recordings, more-or-less continuous grooves are cut in a spiral and the volume is proportional to the depth of the cut. In the digital version of this process, distinct pits are cut instead of continuous grooves. Optical disks are used primarily to record digital data; however, the pits or other changes to the recording surface are read with a laser, not a physical needle. As such, about one thousand to 10 thousand times more information can be shoehorned onto a 12-inch disk.

CD-ROM discs (the spelling varies from disks) use this modern technology and differ from WORM optical disks in that the recording usually must be done in a manufacturing setting, rather than in a jukebox drive. Unfortunately, although the idea of using a laser is all but universal, the method of recording the data is not. For the most part, disks that were recorded with different technologies are not interchangeable. Keep this in mind when designing a large integrated system. The choice for the pilot can restrict many future options:

- **Bimetallic alloy.** This process mixes two adjacent materials into a third that is metallurgically different from the two sources. Hence, the alloy will react differently to the laser beam and send back a different signal.

- **Ablative.** In this process, a hole is dug or etched in the recording surface with two variations. In one, the material is in effect removed. In the other, it forms a lip like a crater. The reflected laser beam returns either out of phase or is less coherent.

- **Dye based.** This is similar to the ablative method, but it stretches the configuration of a layer of dye. It creates rather than digs pits. In the process, it changes the alignment of the reflected laser beam.

- **Thermal bubble.** This is a variation of the dye based, in which the dye is raised rather than pushed (thus creating a microscopic air pocket of sorts). Again, this reflected laser beam is from one reflected from a clean surface.

Rewritable optical disks use variations of these techniques so that the changes are less permanent. That is, the surface must be capable of being easily restored to its original clean form and still be stable.

Three techniques are common for rewritable optical disks. The *magneto-optical technique* reorients the polarity of a laser beam and the *phase-change technique* reduces the reflectivity of the recording surface. Both changes can be reversed. The *dye-polymer technique* is similar to WORM bubbles, except that the bubbles can be deflated. Figure C-4 shows the relationships between these techniques as applied to WORM and rewritable disks.

C.5 Indexing and relational database structure

Many, if not most, documents in an image systems are hierarchically organized. That is, pages are part of documents, which are part of folders, which are part of some higher-level categorization, and so on. This structure is somewhat similar to the hierarchical structure for databases. The access process

Description	WORM disks	Rewritable disks
Physics The atomic structure is rearranged so that laser beams will be reflected differently.	Impractical. Any change of this nature is either easy to reverse or it cannot be limited to small enough an area.	Ideal in the sense that it takes the least work on the part of the laser and is easier to erase.
Chemistry This involves a chemical or metallurgical change to the material used on recording surfaces.	Works very well for WORM disks. The bimetallic alloy "welding" process is the most common application.	Impractical for rewritable disks. The change cannot be reversed without damaging the surrounding areas.
Geometry This changes the geometry rather than the composi-tion or the innards of the surface.	The most popular technology for WORM disks with three variants: ablative, dye based, thermal bubbles.	It works when the flexible dye is used, and is less subject to early decay.

Fig. C-4. Optical disks use several technologies that are seldom interchangeable. Still, all are based on a common principle: the recording surface is modified so that reflected laser beams differ than when reflected from a clean surface.

descends by layers until it locates the desired image. By contrast, the relational database structure puts every record on an equal footing. The great advantage is that it makes the integration of disparate databases easier. If large-scale integration is the goal, this seemingly arcane point will loom large (FIG. C-5).

C.6 Network characteristics

The only significant problem that image records have imposed on networks and communications arises from long record lengths. Moreover, the only negative effect in practice is that access times can be increased to an intolerable length. Unfortunately, that is problem enough for any image system that depends on rapid access—especially if it is used in conjunction with customer telephone calls.

Hierarchical database structure

Each level can be reached only by descending down the logical tier of a hierarchical index.

Relational database structure

All records have the same index fields. Access to any level is via direct lookup in the index.

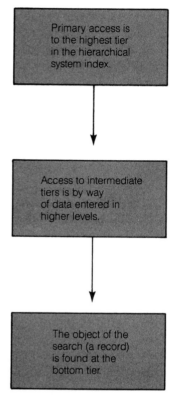

Primary access is to the highest tier in the hierarchical system index.

Access to intermediate tiers is by way of data entered in higher levels.

The object of the search (a record) is found at the bottom tier.

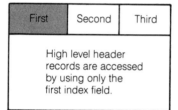

First	Second	Third

High level header records are accessed by using only the first index field.

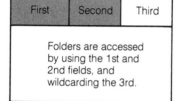

First	Second	Third

Folders are accessed by using the 1st and 2nd fields, and wildcarding the 3rd.

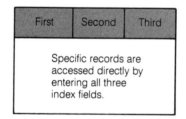

First	Second	Third

Specific records are accessed directly by entering all three index fields.

Fig. C-5. Over the last ten years, the logical flexibility of the relational structure has taken precedence over the neat lines of the hierarchical model. Image processing seems to be going through the same learning process.

The problem arises from two mutually reinforcing factors. The first is that existing network lines (owned or leased) are often used to near capacity. The second is that long image records severely overtax the remaining capacity. An analogy would be an attempt to transport 100 additional passengers in a 400-seat aircraft that is already booked for 390 people. Obviously, the additional passengers will be forced to wait.

To make matters worse most shared communications lines are based on packet-sharing. Every message is subdivided into neat packets of, say, 512 bytes, and sent along with everyone else's traffic. The result is that 3,000-byte records get through without much delay, but 60,000-byte records can require some time. Also, if the record is part of a folder that has photos or other picture-type images in it, the bitstream can easily exceed one million bytes. It doesn't take much imagination to realize the consequences of this electronic bloat.

Accordingly, the network service can be upgraded or the database can be distributed. The service is usually upgraded by increasing the bandwidth. Wider bandwidths in effect provide more channels. Although the flow of packets remains constant, the faucet, so to speak, has been opened much wider. Another solution is to lease or install dedicated lines. The latter solution is by far the most expensive, unless the traffic is dense enough to keep it busy 24 hours per day. An alternative approach is to distribute data (or leave it distributed if that is the way it is collected). In this way, communication delays in sending updates are immaterial, and sometimes it is cheaper and simpler to ship the optical disks.

The optimum solution for a specific organization will depend on its own situation and what the numbers "say." With respect to local-area networks, however, the answer will almost always be to install a new one that supports the image-system workstations. Only in rare cases will existing nets do the job, and even then they can require so much rewiring that the adaptation will become counterproductive.

C.7 Conversion of existing paper records

Almost every organization that installs an image system must face the existing files. Should they be converted to image records—called *backfile conversion?* If so, how far back? The answer will vary with the circumstances based on the operation of a number of factors:

- **Holding period and use of active records.** Existing records that are kept in active status for only a year are less likely to be converted than, say, if they are kept for seven years (all other things being equal). Usually, however, the "other things" are not equal—the other factor is usage. When existing records are accessed frequently, then dual systems, manual and automated, must be maintained until the newest of the existing records can be pushed into inactive status.

- **Extent to which older and newer records are related.** Records old and new can have a strong logical relationship, irrespective of the access requirements for former. Files on personnel and policyholders are good examples. Without backfile conversion in these circumstances, the risk for transaction disconnects is high.

- **Cost and potential disposition of space.** The more critical the need for space, or alternatively the more that can be saved by getting rid of it, the more backfile conversion repays the investment. Still, it is easy to underestimate or overestimate the magnitude of this factor.

- **Logic of the indexes.** Changing the indexing logic for the automated system markedly from the old manual system is also a strong incentive for backfile conversion.

Irrespective of the outcome of the analysis, several points apply to most situations. First, the process of backfile conversion is not normally good training for operators. However, once on-line, the records can be used to support training. For this reason, many companies use service bureaus for backfile conversion. Second, manual systems generally work well, except for the limits imposed by relying on single copies of paper records. Thus, unless processing requirements and/or financial leverage suggest otherwise, the better decision could be to let it alone. Keep in mind that the issue increasingly becomes academic as each day passes.

C.8 The power curve of access speed

Improving image record access speed adheres to an early-rising power curve, but above a certain point it can quickly wipe out the entire investment return. For example, if a delay of seven or eight days is acceptable for sending a parcel across the country, parcel post is fine and economical. For a somewhat higher cost, the delay will be reduced to two or three days. For an even higher price overnight delivery service is available.

If that is too slow, the parcel can be taken to an airport and put aboard the next flight out. At that point the price is about $50 (much higher if accompanied by a courier) or about 10 times that for parcel post. If that is still too slow, you can charter a supersonic transport or you can build a cross-country parcel shipment system as an enlarged version of a physics particle accelerator, for 10 billion dollars or more.

Obviously, this analogy has been pushed to a ridiculous extreme, but only to make a point. Image retrieval can be reduced significantly for only marginal costs up to a point. Jukeboxes can be loaded with the maximum number of drive units. Local-area networks can be upgraded. Electronic "cards" can be (and usually are) substituted for software emulation. Larger intended networks can be subdivided. Magnetic storage can be used for the most active records. And so forth and so on. In practice, most installations take maximum advantage of these economies.

However, what if all of this technology causes a maximum wait of 15 seconds for access to an on-line file, and the boss decides that that time needs to be cut in half or reduced to 5 seconds. To do this, all optical disks would be maintained in a drive unit (or alternatively on magnetic disk, a more volatile state). If a jukebox can hold 288 disks, but no more than 4 drive units, the number of drive units must be increased by a factor of 72. That improvement would raise the price several million dollars.

For image systems, the bottlenecks are jukebox mechanisms and inadequate wide-area communications (when applicable). Thus, when access realtime is truly critical, it is better to use some form of caching for the most intense periods of access (per record) and accept the economies for the balance.

Appendix D

A spreadsheet model for project analysis

All knowledge resolves itself into probability.
David Hume

The spreadsheet model outlined in this appendix is a rudimentary decision support system for macro analysis of image processing opportunities. It is a series of four screens for input data on numbers, dates, values, costs, parameters, and switches for various optional factors. It calculates return on investment (ROI) based on three scenarios: worst-case, best-case, and the median. The ROI tables include a macro-invoked supporting graph, which comprises a decision support model by indicating the outcomes from different inputs.

The model has been designed to work on Lotus 1-2-3 version 2.2, although it will probably work just as well on the earlier 2.01 version. And of course it can be exported to versions 3.0 and 3.1 as is. What's more, in these three-dimension versions, the model can be copied to any number of other layers (up to 255 and subject to computer available memory). In this way, the different ROIs for different inputs can be seen in rapid sequence, and spreadsheet jockeys can develop overarching logic that automatically updates the various models based on meta-factors.

Users are free to use and modify the logic of this model (assuming that the spreadsheet software is licensed) without violating the copyright of this book.

D.1 Structure

The model comprises nine screenfuls of cell entries. The first screen (FIG. D-1) consists entirely of label (comment) entries for using the model. The remaining eight screens are depicted in perspective (FIG. D-2). As with most spreadsheets, the changes to input data automatically recalculate all formulas. In this

- Enter '|| in I1, then range copy I1 to I1..I100.
- Enter @**ABS(@INT(C3))** in C4, then name the cell **START**.
- Enter @**IF(H3 = 1000,1000,1)** in H4, then name the cell **FACTOR**.
- Format C4 for **Fixed,0** and format H4 for **Currency,0**

D.2 Capital and upfront costs screen

These costs include capital items and one-time expenses, such as the prepara-
tion of software and consulting fees (if any) necessary to implement an image
system. *Cost data* includes minimum and maximum values. *Quantity data* is
self explanatory, and setting the quantity to zero eliminates it from the calculations.

Data is entered for each of five years, as applicable, except that lease can-
cellation offset savings for the second through fifth years default to the first-
year entry.

Enter the following label and initial value data:

A21: CAPITAL & UPFRONT COSTS—Enter data and update percentage
depreciable.
A22: ' Note: For StopLease entries, subsequent years default to same value.

A24: ITEM	B24: '		Depreciable	
A25: Planning	C25: "na	D25: 20	E25: 0
A26: Computer Hardware	C26: "na	D26: 600	
A27: Networks	C27: .9	D27: 100	
A28: Workstations	C28: .9	D28: 120	
A29: Micrographics	C26: .9	D29: 0	
A30: Software	C30: "na	D30: 200	
A31: Initial Training	C31: "na	D31: 30	
A32: Set-Up Costs	C32: "na	D32: 100	
A33: Consulting Fees	C33: "na	D33: 0	
A34: Other	C34: 0	D34: 0	
A35: Other	C35: 0	D35: 0	
A36: OFFSETTING COSTS, IF ANY			
A37: Sale	C37: "na	D37: 50	E37: 0
A38: StopLease	C38: "na	D38: 10	
A39: StopLease	C39: "na	D39: 0	

- Enter **+ $START** in D24; **+ $START + 1** in E24;
  + $START + 2 in F24; **+ $START + 3** in G24; **+ $START + 4** in H24.
- Format C26..C35 for **Percent,0**.
- Format D25..H39 for **Currency,0**.
- Range copy E25 to E25..H35
- Range copy E37 to E37..H37
- In E38 enter **+ D38**
- Range copy E38 to E38..H39

D.3 Operating costs screen

Operating cost data is broken down into copying and other expenses. Data is
entered for the current and for the first year of the new system period. Subse-

quent year data defaults to the first year data, but it can be overwritten in every case.

Enter the following label and initial value data:

```
A41:  OPERATING COSTS—Enter current and first-year data. Note: subsequent
A42:  ' year data defaults to previous year data but may be overwritten.
A44:  Cost per copy for copying:        D44: .04
                                   C46: "Current
A47:  ITEM              --------------------------------------------------------------
A48:  Copies per Year  C48: 40000   D48: 15000
A50:  Copies per Year  C50: 0       D50: 15
A51:  Copies per Year  C51: 20      D51: 10
A52:  Copies per Year  C52: 20      D52: 10
A53:  Copies per Year  C53: 10      D53: 30
A54:  Copies per Year  C54: 5       D54: 25
A55:  Copies per Year  C55: 8       D55: 10
A56:  Copies per Year  C56: 0       D56: 0
A57:  Copies per Year  C57: 0       D57: 0
A58:  Copies per Year  C58: 0       D58: 0
```

- Range copy D24..H24 to D46.
- Format D44 for **Currency,2**.
- Format C48..H48 for **Comma,0**.
- Format C50..H58 for **Currency,0**.
- In E50 enter **+D50**, then range copy E50 to E50..H58.
- Range copy B43..B46 to B48..B51, and again to B53..B56
- Name D44 **COPYCOST**

D.4 Operating savings screen

This screen provides input for both personnel and space savings data. The upper half includes input for cost and percentage factors. The lower half is for entering numbers of personnel and space footage. The second and subsequent years default to the previous year.

```
A61:  OPERATING SAVINGS—Enter current and first-year data. Note: subsequent
A62:  ' year data defaults to previous year data but may be overwritten.
A64:  Average Salary Clerks:       D64: 16000  F64: SPACE UNIT COSTS
A65:  Average Salary Supervisors   D65: 30000  G65: Lease H65: Overhead
A66:  Average Salary Others        D66: 40000  F66: Type A: G66: 15 H66: 5
A67:  Benefits Percent Add-On      D67: 32     F67: Type B: G67: 9  H66: 4
A68:  Overhead Percent Add-On      D68: 10     F68: Type C: G67: 4  H66: 3
```

```
                              C70: "Current
A71:  ITEM              -------------------------------------------------
A72:  Number of Clerks   C72: 25      D72: 12
A73:  Number of Spvsrs   C73: 6       D73: 2
A74:  Number of Others   C74: 1       D74: 2
A76:  Type A Footage     C76: 10000   D76: 3000
A77:  Type B Footage     C77: 20000   D76: 3000
A78:  Type C Footage     C78: 0       D76: 0
```

	A	B	C	D	E	F	G	H
1	Return on investment analysis model							
2								
3	Enter first year:		1992		Enter units ($1 or $1000):			$1,000
4	Confirmation:		1992		Confirmation:			$1,000
5								
6	Screen shifting and graph							
7		1. Press PGDN or PGUP to shift among input screens.						
8		2. Press HOME followed by right TAB to shift to ROI screen.						
9		3. Press F10 to display ROI graph. Press ESC to return to data.						
10								
11	Technical notes							
12		A. Enter only positive numbers.						
13		B. Do not inflate inputs; the model computes inflation.						
14		C. For percentage data, include percent sign.						
15		D. Defaults can be overwritten, but do not resave to original						
16		file. That would erase default formulas.						
17		E. Each screen has its own instructions.						
18		F. The model should be initially entered in a spreadsheet with						
19		the test input values and other defaults shown.						
20								

Fig. D-1. The instruction screen assumes that all spreadsheet columns are set to the default of nine spaces and should be entered in the upper left screen. Shifting among all screens is based on using the PgUp, Tab, PgDn, Tab, Shift-Tab, and Home keys.

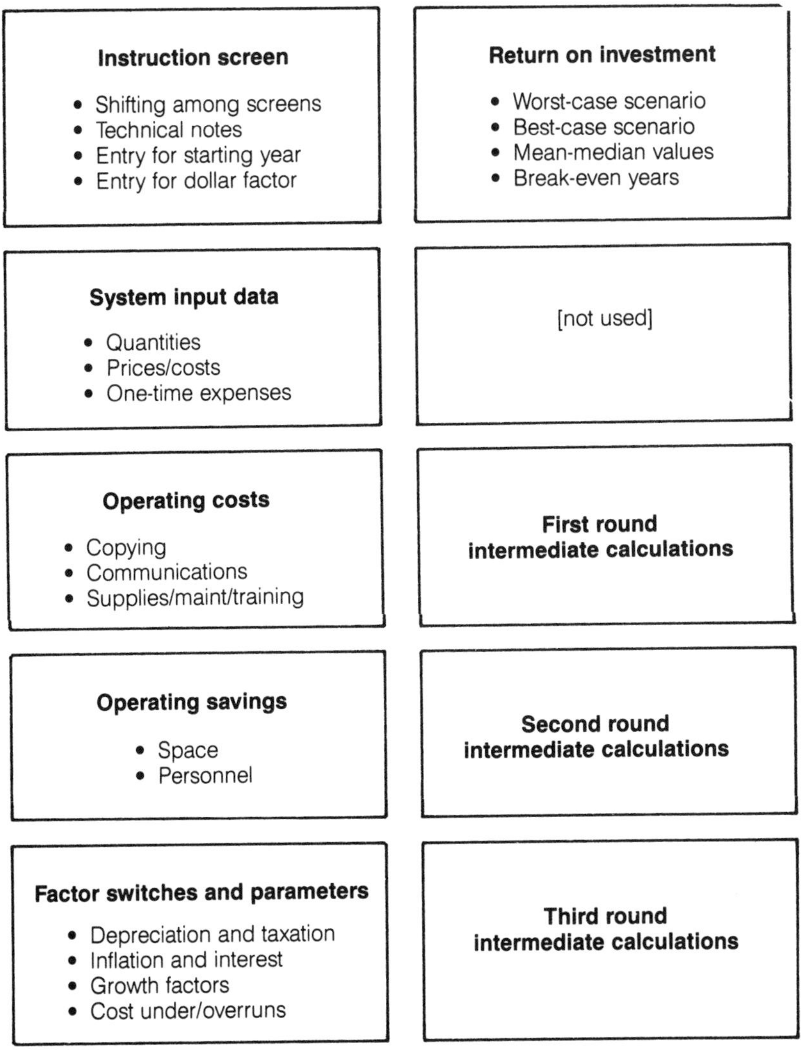

Instruction screen

- Shifting among screens
- Technical notes
- Entry for starting year
- Entry for dollar factor

Return on investment

- Worst-case scenario
- Best-case scenario
- Mean-median values
- Break-even years

System input data

- Quantities
- Prices/costs
- One-time expenses

[not used]

Operating costs

- Copying
- Communications
- Supplies/maint/training

**First round
intermediate calculations**

Operating savings

- Space
- Personnel

**Second round
intermediate calculations**

Factor switches and parameters

- Depreciation and taxation
- Inflation and interest
- Growth factors
- Cost under/overruns

**Third round
intermediate calculations**

Fig. D-2. These are the nine screens for the spreadsheet model (minus the graphics-display macro). The sequence of the intermediate calculation screens modifies each previous screen with additional factors in order to facilitate user modifications.

case, there is little need to activate the manual recalculation feature to save processing time.

Set-up a clean spreadsheet as follows:

- Change the width of column I to 2 spaces.
- Change the width of column J to 16 spaces.
- Enter \ = in A20, then range copy A20 to A20..P20.
- Range copy A20..P20 to A40, to A60, to A80, and to A100.

- Format D64..D66 for **Currency,0**.
- Format G66..H68 for **Currency,2**.
- Format D67..D68 for **Percent,0**.
- Range copy D46..H46 to D70
- Format C72..H74 for **Fixed,0**.
- Format C76..H78 for **Comma,0**.
- Name D67 **BENEFITS**
- Name D68 **OVERHEAD**

D.5 Factors and parameters screen

This final input section provides optional "switches" for anticipated increases to market share, lost opportunity costs, inflation, and other items of a subjective nature that nevertheless entail some aspect of quantification. The features are activated by changing the default 0 entries to another value.

Enter the following label data:

A81: FACTORS & PARAMETERS—A rate other than 0 turns the feature on.
A83: Average Depreciation Rate: D83: .1
A84: Average Depreciation Rate: D84: .25
A86: Average Depreciation Rate: D86: .06
A87: Average Depreciation Rate: D87: .07
A89: Average Depreciation Rate: D89: .03
A90: Average Depreciation Rate: D90: .01
A91: Average Depreciation Rate: D91: .8
A93: Cost/Savings Under/Overrun: D93: .3
E83: The formulas in the model combine
E84: tax and depreciation calculations.
E86: Each factor is applied in succes-
E87: sion cumulatively.
E89: These rates are combined into a
E90: single growth factor applied
E91: cumulatively.
E93: In final ROI for best/worse cases.
E94: '---
   D95: 1   E95: 2   F95: 3   G95: 4   H95: 5
A96: Compound Cumulative Factors
   C97: Inflation
   C98: Interest
   C99: Growth

- Range format D83..D93 for **Percent,0**.
- Range copy D70..H70 to D96
- Range format D97..H99 for **Fixed,2**.
- In D97 enter **(1 + D86)^D95**
- In D98 enter **(1 + D87)^D95**
- In D99 enter **(1 + (D89 + D90)*D91)^D95**
- Range copy D97..D99 to D97..H99
- Name D83 **DEP**
- Name D84 **TAX**
- Name D93 **OVERRUN**

D.6 Intermediate calculation screens

All calculations between the input data, the switches, and the summary return-on-investment time table are entered in three progressive screens. It should be noted, however, that the progression of screens does not correspond to the "progression" of input screens, but rather to the logical progression of the calculations.

Enter the following label data:

J41: FIRST COMPUTATION—This section computes the summaries of input data.
    K3: "Current
J44: Start-Up Costs
J45: Offsetting Costs
J46: Total Start-Up
J47: (depreciable)
J49: Operating Costs
J51: Clerical Pers.
52: Supervisors
53: Other Personnel
J54: Total Personnel
J56: Lease A
J57: Lease B
J58: Lease C
J59: Total Lease
J61: SECOND COMPUTATION—This section computes the basic ROI.
    K63: "Current

J64:	Start-Up Costs	K64:	"na
J65:	Net Oper. Costs	K65:	"na
J66:	Total Costs	K66:	"na
J67:	(depreciable)	K67:	"na
J69:	Net Pers Savings	K69:	"na
J70:	Net Space Saving	K70:	"na
J71:	Total Savings	K71:	"na
J73:	Basic ROI	K73:	"na

J75: THIRD COMPUTATION—This adjusts for depreciation and taxation.

J77:	Costs	K77:	"na
J78:	Savings	K78:	"na
J79:	ROI	K79:	"na

J81: FOURTH COMPUTATION—This factors for cumulative inflation.
    K83: "Current
J88: FIFTH COMPUTATION—This factors for lost opportunity/savings interest.
J94: SIXTH COMPUTATION—This factors for the cumulative growth factor.

- Range copy K77..L79 to K83, then to K89, then to K95.
- Range copy D46..H46 to L43, then to L63, then to L83.
- Range format M44..P98 for **Currency,0**.
- Range format L49..L59 for **Currency,0**.

- In L44 enter **@SUM(D25..D35)**
- In L45 enter **@SUM(D37..D39)**
- In L46 enter **+L44−L45**
- In L47 enter **+D26*$C26+D27*$C27+D28*$C28+D29*$C29+D34*$C34+D35*$C35**

- Range copy L44..L47 to L44..P47
- In K49 enter **+C48*$COPYCOST/$FACTOR + @SUM(C50..C58)**
- In K51 enter **+C72*$D64/$FACTOR + @SUM($BENEFITS + $OVERHEAD)**
- Range copy K51 to K51..K53
- In K54 enter **@SUM(K51..K53)**
- In K56 enter **+C76*($G66 + $H66)/$FACTOR**
- Range copy K56 to K56..K58
- In K59 enter **@SUM(K56..K58)**
- Range copy K51..K59 to K51..P59

- In L64 enter **+L46**
- In L65 enter **+L49**
- In L66 enter **+L64 − L65**
- In L67 enter **+L47**
- In L69 enter **+$K54 − L54**
- In L70 enter **+$K59 − L59**
- In L71 enter **+L69 + L70**
- In L73 enter **+L71 − L66**
- In L77 enter **(L66 − L67*$DEP)/(1 + $TAX)**
- In L78 enter **+L71*(1 − $TAX)**
- In L79 enter **+L78 − L77**
- Range copy L64..L79 to L64..P79

- In L84 enter **+L77*D$97**
- In L85 enter **+L78*D$97**
- In L86 enter **+L85 − L84**
- In L90 enter **+L84*D$98**
- In L91 enter **+L85*D$98**
- In L92 enter **+L91 − L90**
- In L96 enter **+L90*D$99**
- In L97 enter **+L90*D$99**
- In L98 enter **+L97 − L95**
- Range copy L84..L98 to L84..P98

D.7 Return-on-investment screen and graph

This screen is a summary of the third intermediate calculation screen. It also computes the worst-case and best-case ROI and the year of the first breakeven point (noting that in a few cases, the curve could turn downwards and nullify the breakeven).

Enter the following label data:

J1:   RETURN ON INVESTMENT—In a few cases, a breakeven can be nullified
      K3: BreakEven
J4:   Worst Case
J5:   Median Data
J6:   Best Case
J8:   FACTORS AND PARAMETERS
J10: Item ———— Percent ———— Factors ————
J11: Depreciation   M11:   same
J12: Taxation

J13:   Under/Overrun
J14:   Inflation
J15:   Interest
J16:   Steady Growth   M16:   same
J17:   Market Growth
J18:   Profitability
J19:   Growth Factor

- Range copy M11 to M11..P13.
- Range copy M16 to M16..P18
- Range copy L43..P43 to M3.
- Format M4..P6 as **Currency,0**.
- Format L4..L18 as **Percent,0**.
- Format M11..P19 as **Fixed,2**.
- In L4 enter **+L97*(1 – $OVERRUN) – L96*(1 + $OVERRUN)**
- In L5 enter **+L98**
- In L6 enter **+L97*(1 + $OVERRUN) – L96*(1 – $OVERRUN)**
- Range copy L4..L6 to L4..P6
- In K11 enter **@IF(DEP = 0,"OFF",DEP)**

Make the following edits in the range K12..K18.

- In K12 change both cell references to **TAX**
- In K13 change both cell references to **OVERRUN**
- In K14 change both cell references to **+D97**
- In K15 change both cell references to **+D98**
- In K16 change both cell references to **D89**
- In K17 change both cell references to **D90**
- In K18 change both cell references to **D91**

- In L11 enter **@IF(DEP = 0,"OFF",1 + DEP)**
- Range copy L11 to L11..L13

Make the following edits in the range L12..L13.

- In L12 change both cell references to **TAX**
- In L13 change both cell references to **OVERRUN**

- In L14 enter **+D97**
- Range copy L14 to L14..P15

- In L16 enter **@IF(D89 = 0,"OFF",1 + D89)**
- Range copy L16 to L16..L18
- Range format for Percent (0 decimals): J8..N11 and J12
- In L19 enter **+D99**
- Range copy L19 to L19..P19.

- In K4 enter **@IF(L4 > 0,$START,@IF(L4 + M4 > 0,$START + 1,@IF(L4 + M4 + N5 > 0,$START + 2,@IF(L4 + M4 + N4 + O4 > 0,$START + 3,@IF(L4 + M4 + N4 + O4 + P4 > 0,$START + 4," NONE")))))**.
- Range copy K4 to K4..K6.

D.8 Test data

The trial inputs should generate the following ROI. For this example, all dollar data was entered and displayed in thousands:

	BreakEven	1992	1993	1994	1995	1996
Worst Case	1994	− $911	$425	$497	$582	$681
Median Data	1993	$389	$692	$810	$948	$1,110
Best Case	1992	$134	$959	$1,123	$1,314	$1,538

For the graph, use type **LINE** and group data **J2..M5 rowwise**. In Lotus version 2.01, J2..J5 would be the X data; K2..K5 the A data; L2..L5 the B data; and M2..M5 the C data.

Appendix E

Association for Information and Image Management

*Good order is the foundation
of all good things.*

Edmund Burke

The world of data processing is rife with trade and professional associations. Accordingly, much of the progress that should emanate from them lacks coordination. Thus far, image processing has been spared that problem. Almost all of the trade and professional work is led by a single organization, the Association for Information and Image Management (AIIM).

AIIM was established in 1943 (originally as the National Micrographics Association). Because micrographics was generally considered to be outside the mainstream of data processing, AIIM (and its NMA predecessor) was regarded as a peripheral association in the world of automation. Then image processing burst on the scene, and within a few years it became AIIM's dominant interest. Membership and the attendance at the annual trade show zoomed. Given this accelerating interest in imaging, AIIM could well become the most important trade association in the business.

E.1 Mission, goals, and organization

The mission of AIIM is: to promote and advance the development and use of systems, services, and technologies that store, retrieve, and manipulate images of documents, to increase the effectiveness of public and private organizations.

This mission has been translated into six goals:

- To be recognized as the expert in the storage, retrieval, integration and management of document images to increase the effectiveness of information management.

- To accelerate industry growth by promoting the development and use of information and image management systems and services in the support of user business objectives.

- To be recognized by the members as being highly responsive to their needs.

- To be the association that attracts the diverse professional-user communities that are involved with the implementation and use of information and image management systems.

- To be the association that attracts companies and individuals that are producing and marketing I&IM systems, services, and technologies.

- To maintain the capability to achieve the mission and goals of AIIM, including physical facilities, staff, volunteer leadership, and a strong financial position.

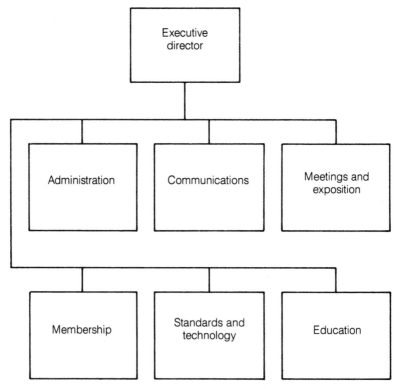

Fig. E-1. AIIM is organized into six divisions: Education is the newest and Standards and Technology is probably the most influential among professionals. The work of Meetings and Exposition is the best known by way of the annual trade shows.

These six goals have been further refined into 33 objectives—most of which are carried by a specific organizational element of AIIM. How well these goals have been achieved can be marked by the more than 500 trade members and six thousand individual members. These figures are remarkable considering that the first commercial image system in the United States did not become operational until 1985. To accommodate that membership, AIIM is organized into six divisions (FIG. E-1). Of these, the Education division is the newest and the Standards-and-Technology division is probably the best known among senior professionals in the field.

Although image processing now overshadows micrographics in terms of publicity, the latter still stores more records and continues to grow. AIIM continues to serve that side of the house as strongly as imaging, and moreover has compiled a remarkable record in establishing standards (both national and international) for this technology. That experience paid off handsomely when it came time to repeat the performance for imaging.

E.2 Annual trade show

The annual trade show is the main event in the life of AIIM (FIG. E-2). It is usually held in the spring of each year in a major city (e.g., Chicago in 1990 and Washington, D.C. in 1991). Micrographics continues to be a mainstay, but no one denies that image systems have cornered the market of public and business interests. Imaging offers solutions that were beyond the reach of micrographics or were beyond that reach until the advent of image processing.

Fig. E-2. The AIIM trade show is not yet as popular as COMDEX, but attendance has been growing at a phenomenal rate.

E.3 Resource center

The resource center at AIIM is probably the most comprehensive and up-to-date collection of references on image processing in the world. More than 14 thousand references are indexed there and virtually all of the more popular books and articles are in hardcopy. Still, the resource center is not a lending library. It is intended for research and reference work while visiting the AIIM offices in Silver Spring, Maryland (Suite 1100, 1100 Wayne Avenue).

Glossary

The problem with most glossaries is that the individuals who are versed in the field use technical dictionaries instead, while those who are new to the field find that most of the terms are defined by other terms in the same glossary. In this glossary some of the similar terms are grouped together.

Address, annotation An *address* refers to a physical or logical location on a storage medium. An *annotation* (or *markup*) is a separate image (or text which can be used to generate a vector image) that can be superimposed over an existing image to form a new one. Neither the old record nor its address is changed, but the resulting combination can be stored as a new image in a new location.

Application programming interface Junctures in software that link systems or vendor software with a program written for one or more specific installation requirements.

Archival, backup, recover The term *archival* refers to records that can be stored reliably for a long time (5 to 100 years). A *backup* is a second copy of an existing record. *To recover* means to restore data from a backup record to or as the primary record. Some users restrict the term *archival* to backup copies.

Attributes, indexes, indices, linkage An *index* is a set of matching numbers and values that given an input value or number, can locate the electronic record corresponding to the input (sometimes called a *key field* or a *handle*). Specific entries in an index are called *indices*, but the term is rarely used in practice. *Attributes* are additional pieces of data or information associated with records that can be added to the record, stored in the index table, or in a separate file. *Linkage* is a generic term that describes how well (or how poorly) records and files are accessible and/or relatable.

Bandwidth, packets, packet switching, protocol These terms describe aspects of communications networks, primarily (in practice) wide-area networks. *Bandwidth* refers to the number of traffic channels that are available in a line. If more lines are available, the same amount of traffic can get through in a shorter time. *Packets* are equal subdivisions of a bitstream for "time sharing" on communications lines. *Packet switching* refers to the mechanics of this time sharing, and a *protocol* is a program that controls or manages message traffic.

Bilevel, halftone, graytone, color, continuous tone, spectral type All five terms refer to the logical composition of the dots/pixels that represent an image system. A *bilevel* is any image that consists of one background color and one foreground color. A *halftone* is a bilevel that is used to create the appearance of shades of gray by grouping pixels into tiny matrixes and then using from 0 to the maximum number of available dots to represent the different shades. A *graytone*, by contrast, produces actual shades of gray by setting aside at least four bits per pixel. Different shades of gray are recorded (and printed) based on the number stored in that set of bits. *Color* is threefold graytone, that is one set of bits per primary color per pixel. *Continuous tone* is a generic term that comprises both graytone and color. Collectively, these descriptions fit under the general term, *spectral type*.

Bar codes, coded data, OCR, NOCR *Coded data* is the generic term that encompasses specific techniques for entering symbols of one kind or another and the ability of a scanner to recognize the pattern and translate that pattern into a unit of processable data. *Bar codes* are bilevel strips of varying width, the most well-known application is UPC codes. *OCR (optical character recognition)* substitutes readable symbols for bar codes, of which the most widely used application is the printed numbers at the bottom of bank checks. NOCR (neural OCR) is pattern recognition of handwritten symbols.

Bitstream, object record The *object record* is the record of an image, usually but not necessarily, in compressed format. When it is not compressed, the raster scan and the object record are essential the same. *Bitstream* is an informal term that refers to the string of bits in a raster scan or object record—especially in transmission.

CD-ROM, WORM, and Rewritable Disks These are all optical disks. The CD-ROM is read-only (written by the manufacturer). WORM means write-once-read-many. Rewritable means the marks placed on the disk to record information can be nullified and the disk reused. Unlike magnetic disks, it takes two separate operations to do this.

Compression, decompression, lossless, lossy, wrap (and non-wrap)   *Compression* is the process of reducing the length of a raster scan by substituting a logical count of color changes, and *decompression* restores a compressed image to its raster scan. Most compression algorithms are line oriented (*nonwrapped*), but if they continue from line to line, they are *wrapped*. When the decompressed image is identical to the original raster scan, it is *lossless*. When it is not identical, which happens with some compression algorithms used for picture-oriented documents, it is *lossy*.

Data processing, image processing   *Data processing*, and its many synonyms, refers to machine processing of character and numerical data. *Image processing*, and its many synonyms, refers to the scanning, compression, storage, decompression, and display of images. However, the processing of data that is associated with image records is not always called data processing.

Document, file, folder, frame, image, record, page, storage hierarchy   These terms, and several others, refer to the hierarchy by which image data is stored. The definitions tend to vary with different vendors, and also vary between data processing and image processing systems. In general, however, a *document* is a physical entity that has one or more pages (e.g., an insurance policy, a book, a letter, or set of blueprints). A *folder* is a collection of related documents (e.g., an electronic personnel folder). A *page* is a single page of a document (one side of it) and a *frame* is that portion of a page that can be viewed on one screen at one time. Some users suggest that if a display can include two or more documents, then collectively they comprise a frame. The terms *file* and *record* are too loose to be of any utility, unless they are explicitly defined for use in a specific system. However, *storage hierarchy* always refers to the tiers by which material is stored in a system (e.g., page, document, and folder). An *image* usually is the recorded version or facsimile of a document page, but in practice the term is often used to cover the document, the object records, the display on a monitor, and a reprint of the record.

Document generation   This term usually refers to creating a vector image from data on file—typically overlaid on another image, which itself might be a raster image. This term also refers to CAD (computer-assisted drafting or design), especially when an engineering drawing is digitized and then used as input to CAD to create modified drawings.

Emulation, simulation   *Emulation* is the use of a hardware device or software program to bridge the gap between any two elements of a system that would otherwise be incompatible. However, the term is not normally used to describe software that must always be used in systems (e.g., a compiler to translate readable source code into an object code that a computer can execute). *Simulation* is to model or to prototype. For example, communications networks can be tested for peak-load handling capability by electronically simulating heavy message traffic.

FAX, raster image, scanner, vector image   A *scanner* is a device that creates an image of a document. A *FAX* is, in effect, a scanner, that primarily transmits a raster image (usually compressed) without permanent storage. A *raster image* is a document that has been reduced to a series of dots; then, the value of those dots are captured as a bit stream. A *vector image* is created by positioning or using data in some form to create the pixels of an image (e.g., the graphs generated in productivity software).

Giga-, kilo-, mega-, tera-   These prefixes represent factors of a billion, a thousand, a million, and a trillion, respectively. Thus,

Kilobyte   =   1,000 bytes
Megabyte   =   1,000,000 bytes
Gigabyte   =   1,000,000,000 bytes
Terabyte   =   1,000,000,000,000 bytes

Image systems require enormous amounts of memory for storage. Some jukeboxes can store one terabyte of records in active (on-call) status, and a single reel of optical tape can store the same amount in on-the-shelf storage.

Host computer, server   A *host computer* provides the so-called primary computer power or capability to a network of workstations, but this term is something of a misnomer. The use of a host computer can be limited to record storage and retrieval, and microcomputers at the workstations do the bulk of the processing. A *server* is a computer to support workstations, which might or might not be operable without a host computer, depending on the configuration of the system.

Integration   To *integrate* means to link two or more separate elements (in this case of automated systems) in such a way that they begin to operate as if they were parts of a larger system. The term is too general for practical use, however. There are many degrees and objects for integration (e.g. database integrations, standardizations, and network interfaces). The most common integrations in image systems are two or more installations that are integrated with each other and linked with data processing databases.

Landscape orientation, portrait orientation   These terms refer to the direction of the longer dimension of a monitor screen. *Landscape orientation* is horizontal; *portrait* is vertical. The latter is intended to view image documents in full scale. However, some landscape monitors are large enough to display a standard-size document on one side and other data (or a second document) on the other side.

Local-area network, token ring, Ethernet   *Token ring* and *Ethernet* are specific forms of local-area networks. The token ring is so named because each message is loaded with a token and it rides circuit until the station calling for it recognizes the token and accepts the traffic.

Microfiche, microfilm, microform, micrographics   *Microfiche* comprises *microfilm* images arranged on a sheet of like film, but usually thicker. *Microform* is the generic term for both (and also includes *aperture cards*, which are microfilm frames mounted in a punch card or similar). *Micrographics* is an even wider generic term that covers the science and technology of using microforms.

Optical disk, optical disk drive, optical disk library (jukebox), optical tape   An optical disk is similar to a phonograph record because information of any kind is recorded by modifying or marking the recording surface in microscopic units. An optical disk drive is a unit that can "write" and "read" these marks, and a disk library (jukebox) is a machine with one or more drivers and the capacity to hold one or more disks beyond those temporarily inserted in a drive. The mechanism exchanges disks when a call for a record is on a disk and not in the drive. Optical tape is to an optical disk what magnetic tape is to a magnetic disk drive.

Pel, picture element, pixel   A *picture element* is the smallest unit of an image record. The abbreviated terms are *pixel* (pix element) and *pel* (picture element). A dot corresponds in meaning, if not in size, to a pel in printing—especially on a dot matrix or ink jet printer (but not a plotter). The terms pel and pixel are both commonly used and are always interchangeable.

Reduction, resolution, scaled   *Resolution* refers to the number of pixels recorded per unit of horizontal length, and the number of rows (rasters) per unit of vertical length. Resolutions of 100×100 and 200×200 are common. *Reduction* is to reduce the size of an image before capture/scanning, or to reduce the display from the size of the original document. Reductions are proportional unless *scaled*—which means that one dimension is reduced (or enlarged) out of proportion to the other dimension.

Workstation A *workstation* is a set of computer-based elements, almost always linked with other workstations and/or a host computer (or server) by a network. The network collectively allows one or more individuals to work, usually on or with respect to accessible records. The manual equivalent is a desk and the ability to stand and fetch records from a file cabinet. Workstations are all but indispensable for image systems, because imaging is a form of automated records management.

References

Commercial image processing references that are older than three years are either academic tomes or out-of-date technical books of little interest to the general reader. However, some of the newer material is couched in proprietary terms that are coined by vendors. These references are good to read, but they emphasize differences, not similarities. Still, those interested in image processing should invest a few weeks with these references.

CAUTION: some of these references come with industrial-strength prices, ranging up to $1,050. However, AIIM members are offered substantial discounts on many of these references when ordered through the AIIM resource center.

A Comprehensive Guide to Integrated Image Systems. Wang Laboratories, Lowell, Massachusetts, 1989.
One of the best educationally-oriented vendor publications. It is especially strong on vendor-customer relationships and on selecting an initial project for a complex installation.

Automated Interchange of Technical Information. MIL-STD-1840 (available through AIIM).
The Department of Defense has imposed standards for some aspects of image records for its contractors and internal agencies. It provides some insights in how corporations can integrate their own systems.

Buying Electronic Image Management Systems. Robert J. Kalthoff.
This is one of the few books that addresses alternatives and options for buying or leasing the components for an image system. The acquisition process can stretch over a year or more, and it has more pitfalls than are generally publicized. The book brings a new and useful meaning to the maxim "let the buyer beware."

Comparison of Commercially Available Optical Based Document Image Systems.
Deloitte Haskins & Sells, 1989.
This contains more than what the title implies.

"Complex Software Architecture Required for Image Processing." Robert L.
Castle. *Computer Technology Review*, 97-98, 100-101, Summer 1989.
A very good perspective on the increasingly complex software requirements
that sophisticated image systems need.

Computerworld. 65-107, November 5, 1990.
Image processing was the cover subject of this issue. The articles cover most
aspects of image systems.

Conceptual Design Guideline for Optical Disk Document Management Systems,
AIIM Research Report, 1988.
A solid planning reference.

Data Compression, Gilbert Held, John Wiley & Sons, New York, 1988.
Few general managers would want to read this technical book, but because
record length is the pivotal factor in system costs for most installations, a wise
executive will ensure that his technical staff studies this subject.

Datapro Reports on Document Imaging Systems, Datapro Research (a division of
McGraw-Hill), Delran, New Jersey, 1990.
This set of 11 paperback volumes in two binders is probably the best single
source of extensive material on virtually all elements of image processing.

Digital Image Processing: A Systems Approach, 2nd edition. William B. Green.
Association of Information and Image Management, Silver Spring, Mary-
land, 1989.
A good volume on the general subject.

Document Image Processing. A. M. Hendley, et al. National Centre for Information, Great Britain, 1990.
This three volume set seems to offer more insights into the business of image
processing and far and away offers the best set of case studies anywhere. The
reader will need perseverance to plow this tome, but it will be well rewarded.
The publication offers no guarantee that its readers will avoid costly mistakes,
but it's a safe bet those to date have.

"Don't Dump Your Computer Stocks: Image Processing Will Expand the Market Explosively in the Nineties." *Forbes*, 257-264, November 6, 1990.
Although this cover-story article is intended as an overview for the general
Forbes readership, it is significant that image processing has become a mainstream subject for business publications.

Handbook of Optical Memory Systems: Feasibility, Design, Implementation. C. Peter Waegemann. Optical Disk Institute, Newton, Massachusetts, 1990.
An easy-to-read, concise, technical information book that compares various vendor products. This binder-format publication is updated six times a year as part of the first-year purchase price.

IBM Systems Journal. Volume 29, Number 3, Fall 1990.
The entire issue (13 articles, all with excellent illustrations) is devoted to various aspects of image processing, albeit IBM systems.

Imaging Processes and Materials, 8th edition. John M. Sturge, et al, editors. Von Nostrand Reinhold, New York, 1989.
A large-format book and one of the best and most-comprehensive technical references available.

"Image Processing at USAA." Charles A. Plesums. *Mainframe Journal,* June 1990, 8-15.
This is probably the most comprehensive article on image processing in existence, and is a distilled account of the experience of an individual who was (and still is) responsible for fielding the system that shifted image processing from the sidelines to the commercial mainstream.

Image Storage and Retrieval Systems: a New Approach to Records Management. Marc R. D'Alleyrand. Intertext Publications, McGraw-Hill Book Company, 1989.
A good book on the technical options for storing and retrieving image records.

InfoImage Basics: Document Imaging, The Picture of Information. Unisys Corporation, Blue Bell, PA, 1990.
Perhaps the best educationally oriented publication from a vendor. The authors Ted Hoobler and Gary Samartino of Documenta show a high patience and empathy with readers who are struggling to master the technical aspects of image systems. The videotape that accompanies the book is even better.

InfoMap: A Complete Guide to Discovering Corporate Information Resources. Cornelius F. Burk, Jr. and Forest W. Horton, Jr. Prentice-Hall, Englewood Cliffs, New York, 1988.
Much useful data lies buried within an organization. It is often overlooked when installing an automated system. This book helps find it.

Information & Image Management: The State of the Industry 1990. Association of Information and Image Management, Silver Spring, Maryland.
This is an annual compendium published by AIIM, though it is more oriented to vendors and other trade members than it is to customers who have specific requirements in mind.

Legality of Optical Storage. Robert F. Williams, editor. Cohasset Associates, Inc., Chicago, 1990.
Arguably the most comprehensive survey and guide on the admissibility of optically stored records as evidence in legal and regulatory proceedings. It includes state-by-state data and Williams also offers a companion volume on legality of microform storage.

MVS/ESA ImagePlus Planning and Installation Guide. IBM document GC38-2025-0, 1990.
See also the companion volume for the AS/400 ImagePlus configuration, IBM document GC38-2028-0, 1990. Although this volume is solely focused on IBM systems, it provides an excellent overview of the technical problems that must be faced in any installation.

MVS/ESA ImagePlus General Information Manual. IBM Document GC38-2024-0, 1990.
See also the companion volume for the AS/400 ImagePlus configuration, IBM document GC38-2028-0, 1990.
In effect, these are executive summaries of the IBM planning and installation guides cited in the Planning and Installation Guide, plus some commentary aimed at higher levels of management.

1990 Information Management Sourcebook, Association of Information and Image Management, Silver Spring, Maryland.
This annual book provides a complete listing of vendors and consultants in the image technology field and includes descriptive information of services and goods that each makes available.

Optical Disk Document Storage and Retrieval Systems, Barry Cinnamon, Association of Information and Image Management, Silver Spring, Maryland.
Perhaps the best reference on scanners; it is one of the few that provides cost data.

Optical Image Management: Competitive Weapon. Robert J. Kalthoff. Association of Information and Image Management, Silver Spring, Maryland.
As the title implies, this book addresses the strategic advantages of image processing systems more so than most other references, and it is based on an evaluation of many working systems.

Positioning the Information and Image Management Industry for Standards Development in the 1990s. Robert B. Toth. Association of Information and Image Management, Silver Spring, Maryland.
Perhaps the best reference on the challenges and problems of standardization, written under the organization that is in the forefront of the work.

Putting Technology in the Background. Abigail Shaw. *Inform,* June 1990, 34-40.
If a senior executive has time to read only two articles on image processing, this and Plesums' are recommended. If time only exists for one article, read them both anyway. They will convince the reader to read more—both to understand the big picture and to realize why many aspects of the technology should not be glossed over.

Records Management Handbook. Ira Penn, Anne Morddel, et al.
The subject matter of this book is often overlooked when managers rush to install image systems. Image systems automate records management, but they do not eliminate requirements or nuances.

Index

203